SHAWN PHILLIPS'

ABSolution

The Practical Solution for Building Your Best Abs

SHAWN PHILLIPS'

ABSolution

The Practical Solution for Building Your Best Abs

HIGH POINT MEDIA

Empowering People Through Empowering Books

Notice

The ABSolution Program is intended for healthy adults, ages 18 and over. This book is solely for informational and educational purposes and is not medical advice. Please consult a medical or health professional before you begin any new exercise, nutrition, or supplementation program or if you have questions about your health. As individuals differ, their results will differ, even when using the same program.

For information, contact:

High Point Media, LLC

651 Corporate Circle, #206

Golden, CO 80401

tel: 303-273-2900

fax: 303-273-2901

www.HighPointMedia.com

FIRST EDITION

ISBN 0-9720184-0-9

Designed by Craig Korn

Photography by Dennis Lane, David Haskell, and Kal Yee

Printed in the USA

To your health

ACKNOWLEDGMENTS

Building a great body is not easy. And as I recently discovered, neither is writing and producing a book. And if it weren't for the help of some very talented and hard-working people, I would have never achieved my goal by completing this project, much less doing so in a manner that I feel reflects the quality I believe you deserve.

So now, I'd like to acknowledge and express my appreciation to the people who helped me. This includes my mother and father, who gave me both the potential and work ethic to develop this body. I'd also like to thank my brother, Bill, for helping me write this book as well as for his belief in this project and his encouragement. I also express appreciation to my friend and business partner, Steve Adelé, whose support means more to me than he may ever know. A special thanks to Harley Pasternak for his expert advice as well. And to Angie Tsiatsos, thank you for giving me strength when I needed it most. Then there are the extraordinarily talented photographers whose work is featured throughout this book. They are Dennis Lane, David Haskell, and Kal Yee. Thank you, gentlemen.

I'd also like to express my appreciation to the production team at High Point Media: Michael Sitzman, whose patient persistence has been such a comforting factor; Jim Nagle, for his optimism and professionalism; Craig Korn, whose graphic and design excellence has served as an inspiration throughout this process; and Leigh Macdonald-Rauen, for her masterful word processing skills. I'd also like to thank Sue Mosebar for her special attention to detail.

And last, but *not* least, I'd like to thank *you*, the reader, for giving me the chance to share the information I've spent so many years gathering. It's a very special opportunity, one I don't take for granted.

ABSolution

Contents

FOREWORD BY BILL PHILLIPS

Author of the #1 *New York Times* Bestseller, *Body-for-LIFE*

I am *so* happy that you are reading these words in this book at this very moment. In fact, I am downright excited about it! Why? Well, the mere fact that you're hearing what I'm saying right now is proof positive this book, which I have been encouraging my brother Shawn to write for almost four years, is finally done! And, now, you have, at your fingertips, what I believe is the most comprehensive, common sense, straightforward guide available today that specifically addresses the question so frequently asked in today's world of fitness. That question being, "How do I build defined abs?" I can't think of *anyone* more qualified to answer that question than Shawn. He knows this topic inside and out. He knows what works and what doesn't. And he practices what he preaches. He's in shape all year long and even at age 38, he's still making improvements in his physique.

Please allow me to share some "up close and personal" information about my brother so you know more about him before you read the rest of this book. To start with, Shawn and I were born in Golden, Colorado, a small town nestled in the foothills about 15 miles west of Denver. Shawn was born a year and six weeks before me. Our mom has a heart of gold and is so loving. Our dad is one of the smartest people you'll ever meet. Together with our older sister, Shelly, we lived a typical small-town lifestyle as kids. We played sports, got good grades in school, and stayed out of trouble, for the most part. As we became young adults, Shawn and I both began to feel a passion for fitness and muscle build-ing. We worked out together, constantly pushing each other and supporting each other. When I'd work out so hard I'd get sick, he'd drive me home and make me drink orange juice until I could stand up straight again and wasn't pale green. And I'd do the same for him. (Thank goodness we never both got sick on the same day!)

When I was about 20 years old and decided to begin sharing what I had learned about muscle building by starting a newsletter, Shawn was right there with me. In fact, he helped me write articles and develop exercise programs that were featured in my first newsletters, which I started in 1985 with the $180 Shawn and I made mowing lawns around our neighborhood in the summer. The idea was to provide enough helpful information to people who were interested in building muscle and losing fat that subscription revenue would help us pay our tuition for college. The idea worked.

In 1992, we transformed the newsletter into a magazine called *Muscle Media* and Shawn's articles appeared in virtually every issue. Shawn was always in such great shape, so I featured his photos on numerous covers and through-out each magazine. Perhaps the most famous photo of Shawn is the one that appears on the cover of my documentary video *Body of Work*. That photo lifted interest in how he built his incredible abs to a new level and prompted literally

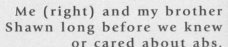
Me (right) and my brother Shawn long before we knew or cared about abs.

thousands of questions about his ab-training "secrets" to come pouring into *Muscle Media* headquarters.

Although Shawn is probably best known publicly for his incredible abs, he is actually better known by his family, close friends, and co-workers as a hard-working, soft-spoken man with a kind heart and a passion for fitness and for designing and developing computer software programs. Over the past decade, he's successfully combined his interests in fitness and technology, first by creating a customized, computer-generated exercise program called Power Systems Technologies that he utilized to design training programs for numerous world-class athletes. More recently, Shawn has created Nutros.com, a high-tech internet site that allows people to research, design, and develop their own customized vitamin and nutritional supplement programs around their specific needs and fitness goals. Shawn was also a key member of the original team that helped me build EAS into the world's leading performance-nutrition company. In late 1999, when I turned EAS over to a new management team, we began the next chapter in our lives. He set out to develop Nutros.com, and I'm building a publishing company called High Point Media with the purpose of empowering people through empowering books.

Shawn still lives in the foothills of Colorado, and his hobbies include snowboarding, mountain biking, reading, and traveling around the world. We often hang out and occasionally still work out together. Shawn is, always has been, and always will be a great friend. And, I am certain you'll find Shawn's advice in this book reflects the values I've seen him demonstrate throughout his life: honesty, integrity, and sincerity.

Once again, I couldn't be happier that this book is finally done! I do hope you enjoy it—it was created especially for *you*. I know firsthand, it is a labor of love.

INTRODUCTION

The question I'm most frequently asked goes something like this, "Shawn, what's your secret—what's the one thing you do differently than everyone else that allowed you to build such great abs?" The one thing, the one thing, the one thing... So many people are looking for the one thing—the secret. Many people think the one thing is some ab-training device like the type you see advertised on television infomercials. It's not. Others would like you to believe that the one thing is some miracle fat-burning pill. It's not. Others would have you believe that the one thing—the big secret—is liposuction or some other quick fix. Once again, it's not.

The fact is, and this is the first and most fundamental lesson of my ABSolution Program, *the one thing* is *everything*! Everything we do affects the way we look and the way we feel. It's when we exercise, how we exercise, and the exercises we do. It's when, what, and how much we eat. It's which vitamins and supplements we nourish our bodies with. It's how much we rest and recover. It's how we think and how we live. It's everything. And, that's what this book is all about. It's about *everything* you need to learn to build your own absolutely fantastic abs.

CHAPTER ONE

My First Lesson

I will never forget my first job in the fitness industry nor the lesson it helped me learn. The year was 1984, and I was a sophomore at Colorado State University, studying computer science. After class, I'd work out at a gym called The Fitness Forum. A lot of students and college athletes worked out there. Many of them wanted to get in great shape for a variety of reasons. And since I was in pretty good shape and had been competing in bodybuilding contests for a few years, people would come to me for advice. I agreed to "personally train" a couple dozen people to help earn extra money to pay my tuition. I figured it would be easy to teach them how to exercise, and in turn, they would start seeing the results they coveted, primarily lower bodyfat, increased muscle definition, and more energy. And so, my journey as a "fitness professional" or "personal trainer" began.

Here's how it worked: each of my "clients" would pay me $25 an hour, and I would meet them at the gym and teach them the proper form and show them what exercises would help them develop their muscles and burn bodyfat. Each workout lasted about 45 minutes. Before each session, we'd talk for a few minutes, and afterwards, I'd spend a little time with them reviewing what we had learned and how they were progressing.

After about a month, about half of my students began to dramatically transform. Their biceps, triceps, and deltoids were more defined; the muscles were separating and popping out; the fat was burning off, and their abs were starting to show. Those clients were becoming more and more energetic, excited, and motivated. They wanted to work hard in the gym. They believed they could succeed. They loved the results and the feeling of being in control of their bodies. Somehow, being able to deliberately recreate the shape of their bodies empowered them and enabled them to feel that they could do well in other areas of their lives. These were my favorite students. I enjoyed working out with them as much as they enjoyed the success they were experiencing.

Now, I need to tell you about the "other half." The clients who were *not* having the same experience as my "better half." The other half of my clients were becoming frustrated. They complained of slow and, in some cases, no results. Each time we met for a workout, they began to look at me with contempt. They literally blamed me for their lack of results. And, since I cared about these people, I really felt awful that they weren't making the same progress as my better half.

At night, after doing my homework, I'd often contemplate what the difference was between my better half and the other half. Some nights, I would lie awake in my dorm room until the early hours of the morning trying to figure it out. I was giving all of them the same exercise instruction. I gave them all the proper nutrition information. In the gym, I was doing everything the same, so why weren't they all experiencing the same results? It didn't make sense. What was I doing wrong?

Then, one night, finally, I realized I wasn't really responsible… not for the success of the better half nor the "failure" of the other half. I realized it had very little to do with me. I realized that even though I might be their personal trainer for an hour a day, *they were their own personal trainers for the other 23 hours!* It was what these people were doing, the decisions they were making, the foods they were eating, their habits and so on when they were not with me that was separating the two groups. The success and/or failure of each of my clients was the responsibility of that person, not me. I played a very small role. And even though I might have

"I realized that even though I might be their personal trainer for an hour a day, *they were their own personal trainers for the other 23 hours!*"

wanted to give myself credit for the success of those clients who were making great gains, and even though I might have felt guilty about the failure of the other half, I realized I was giving myself more credit than I deserved. And that was my first lesson about teaching fitness: I could do only so much. The rest was up to the students. They must decide to do what it takes to get results, not *just* in the gym but in the kitchen and throughout their lives. Working out is not enough. You have to be willing to do *everything* right.

Now, what does this have to do with the ABSolution Program? Well, the fact is, even though I might be somewhat of a "fitness expert," that doesn't mean I have the ability to make you do something *you* haven't *decided* to do. I cannot motivate you to change your body and enjoy all the benefits that go with it if *you* haven't already decided to do so. You see, until you decide to allow the ABSolution Program to work for you, I cannot, in return, guarantee you a positive result. You, not me, determine your success with this program. You are the one who will decide *when* and *why* you do this. I can only show you *how*. I can show you *exactly* how. I can and will show you how to exercise, how to feed your body, how to take advantage of nutritional supplementation, and all the rest. However, I cannot decide for you when or why you give this program the opportunity to work for you as it has for so many others. And that is something I cannot emphasize enough. I can be your "personal trainer" for only so many moments in a day. *You*, ultimately, *are your own personal trainer*. You must be your own success coach. You must be your own motivator. You are the master. *You* are the one who holds the key, not I. Teaching, my job, is the easy part. "Doing," which is your part, is hard.

I'm not going to go on and on with a bunch of rah-rah motivational rhetoric. That's not me. That might be what you'll get from someone else, but that's not what you should expect from me. I'm straightforward. I take a no-nonsense approach to fitness. But, as I learned almost 20 years ago working as a personal trainer at The Fitness Forum in Fort Collins, Colorado, I don't have the power to change you. But you do. *You* have the

power to change your body. No one can give that to you, and no one can take it away. I'm here to empower you by giving you knowledge. Knowledge I have spent many years accumulating. And knowledge that will absolutely, positively enable you to build a better body; sculpt great-looking, muscular abs; and enjoy a healthier, higher quality life.

You and only you can determine if you have a good reason to apply the powerful information in this book. There are a lot of great reasons to do so, though. For example, maybe you're sick and tired of looking the way you look and feeling the way you feel, and you are *ready* to do something about it. That's a good reason to put this program into action. Maybe you're competing in the Body-*for*-LIFE Challenge and want to join my brother Bill's "championship team" and be one of the success stories that inspires others through your example. That's an excellent reason, and one which has

inspired literally hundreds of thousands of people into action. Maybe you've been fired-up, psyched-up, and motivated for months, even years, but you haven't had the knowledge—you haven't had the Program that really works to help you get where you want to go. If so, make no mistake, the ABSolution Program *will* help you get there, *if* you decide to do it. Maybe you're concerned about your health—maybe your doctor has warned that if you don't lose weight and bust that gut, your days on this earth are numbered. Absolutely, that's a heck of a reason to make a change and allow this Program to work for you.

There are *so* many great reasons to get in better shape. What's yours? You must have one, or you wouldn't have invested money to buy this book in the first place, and you wouldn't be investing your valuable time right now to read it. Only you know your reason. I don't know your reason. I can't give you a reason. Only you can make that decision. But I assure you that once you make that decision and once you identify the reason that motivates and inspires you, I will give you the information you deserve—the practical, real facts about how to move forward and create the body you want.

Now, before we go any further, I need to ask, *are you ready?* Are you *truly* ready to do this? Are you ready to work hard, sacrifice little pleasures, and overcome unproductive habits to achieve something great—to build your best body and sculpt your best abs? If so, I encourage you to carefully read the material in this book. I encourage you to put it into action. I encourage you to separate yourself from the "other half" and become a winner. And I encourage you to become the person who you really are *inside*. I want you to be able to look in the mirror in the near future, smile, and beam with pride about the reflection you see. If that's what you want too, please, turn the page, and let's get to work.

CHAPTER **TWO**

The Bigger
Picture

I was being interviewed for a magazine article last year and doing what I often do: answer questions about exercise, nutrition, and getting in shape. The questions are generally the same, and so are the answers. (The truth never changes.) However, about an hour into this discussion, I was asked a question I have *not* answered a hundred times before. In fact, it was a question I hadn't really given much thought to prior to the moment the reporter looked at me, shrugged his shoulders, and asked, "Shawn, in this uncertain and downright frightening post-9/11 new world, why even bother trying to get in shape, much less build rock-hard abs?"

Typically, I answer questions very quickly; as I said, they're so often routine. But this time, the answer didn't come to me right away. I paused, took a deep breath, leaned back in my chair, and gazed out the window. I had to think about it for a few minutes before I found the answer. And when I did, I saw the "bigger picture" like I've never quite seen it before. My perspective had evolved and expanded to a level beyond what I was even aware of. I could see and feel the importance of fitness like never before. So, with clarity and confidence, I looked the reporter in the eye, leaned forward, and shared how I see it…

First of all, taking care of yourself and doing what you can to become as healthy and fit as possible matters *now* more than ever! I believe that with all my heart. I think that a strong nation is made up of strong people; therefore, one thing *each* and *every* person in this country can do to help strengthen America is strengthen themselves. We can all make a difference, but we must start by taking responsibility for ourselves.

Next, there's the economical aspect that impacts our country and each and every one of us. Each year, the United States government spends over $100 billion caring for Americans who didn't take care of themselves. That money goes to treat people who are suffering from obesity and its secondary diseases, such as diabetes, heart disease, vascular disease, and cancer. And when we don't take care of ourselves and allow our bodies to weaken and decay, we can also develop debilitating diseases such as osteoporosis.

A lack of physical strength also contributes to millions of unnecessary injuries each year, which cost billions of dollars in lost productivity as well as medical bills. So, if you just look at it from a fiscal standpoint alone, you can begin to see how vitally important it is to make sure we don't become a burden to our country and its economic resources, especially in this day and age.

Then there's the mental aspect: it's a fact that when you strengthen the body, you strengthen the mind; you strengthen character and courage. Consider how much people today need a healthy way to deal with uncertainty, anxiety, stress, and confusion. And consider the fact that it has been scientifically proven that regular and intense exercise, as well as feeding the body in a healthy manner, helps keep the mind clear, reduces depression, and releases stress. That, in turn, increases our productivity and improves quality of life. And, has there *ever* been a more important time in our nation's history for its citizens to be strong, healthy, and courageous? I don't think there has been.

What I explained to the reporter that day is what I would encourage you to take a look at also. I hope you too can see the bigger picture. I hope you too can see that making time in your life for fitness is not frivolous. I hope you too can see that when you become a stronger, healthier individual, you are improving not just yourself but the lives of those around you, your community, and even your country. That's how I now view the bigger picture. I hope you see it that way too.

"Taking care of yourself and doing what you can to become as healthy and fit as possible matters *now* more than ever!"

CHAPTER THREE

Defining the Target

Let's get real: building your best abs is going to require hard work and sacrifice. That's a fact. But, it's also a fact that the vast majority of ab-training "experts" totally ignore this in their infomercials, ads, articles, and so on. So before we go any further in this book, and before I teach you my ABSolution Program, I need to set the record straight.

The fact of the matter is that in order to develop your *best abs*, you absolutely, positively must develop your *best body*. You must lower your bodyfat and increase your overall muscle definition. You must get in really, *really* great shape. That's the only way you'll ever be able to see your abs.

Becoming so fit that you have defined abs is akin to hitting the bull's eye on the target. It's like swinging for a home run—make that a *grand slam*—in baseball. It's like going for a gold medal in the Olympics.

Make no mistake, defining the target as becoming so fit that your abs are cut is setting your sights high, *very high*. It's not an easy thing to do. In fact, it's downright challenging. However, by the time your abs are in top shape, rest assured your legs are going to be in shape, your arms are going to be lean and strong, your back and shoulders are going to be muscular, and your whole body is going to be fit. And you're going to be healthy on the inside as well. Your heart, lungs, vascular system, immune system... they will all be healthier.

Defining extraordinary health by the condition of the abdominal muscles and the overall physique is not a new idea. It's not a fad. As my brother Bill pointed out in his documentary movie *Body of Work,* building your body is the oldest new idea in self-empowerment. It's an idea that goes back over 2,000 years to the ancient Greeks whose aim was to cultivate a balance between the mind and body, a philosophy ancient Romans would describe with the saying, *"Mens sana in corpore sano,"* which basically means, "A sound mind in a sound body." Their mythological figures, such as Zeus, Apollo, Atlas, and Hercules, to name but a few, were depicted as muscular and strong—they were metaphors of the Greek ideal and philosophy.

In the 15th and 16th centuries during the Renaissance, artists like Leonardo da Vinci and Michelangelo studied the works of the Greeks in an effort to help lift Europe out of the Dark Ages and restore hope, learning, independent thinking, and overall "fitness." Michelangelo, in particular, saw the body as the manifestation of the soul and character. He believed that if the mind were strong and the soul pure, then the figure in the sculpture or painting that represented it should be lean, strong, muscular, and defined. Perhaps that's why so many of Michelangelo's famous works of art, including his painting on the ceiling of the Sistine Chapel of God creating Adam and his sculpture of the Biblical young king David, depict muscular, proportionate figures, with clearly defined abdominal muscles.

The bottom line is when you define the target as sculpting lean and muscular abdominal muscles, you are making the decision to work hard to not just get in good shape but to get in *great shape!* And, when you become so lean and strong that you can see your abs, you'll literally become your own self-created work of art; you will have mastered one of the most important things that you could possibly gain control and command over, and I don't just mean your body, I mean your mind and your character—the essence of who you *really* are.

"Becoming so fit that you have defined abs is akin to hitting the bull's eye on the target."

CHAPTER FOUR

A Step in the Right Direction

"Even the longest journey starts with a single step." I read those words of wisdom many years ago and often found myself repeating them for encouragement during times when I needed to be patient and persistent—to not give up. But, more recently, I've revised this saying to include something I've learned along the way, specifically that most people who hold the aspiration of becoming extraordinarily healthy, fit, and strong don't see the pursuit of that objective as just a "journey." What they want to make is a *successful* journey. They want to get where they want to go as fast as possible. So do I. So the way I now see it is, "A successful journey starts not just with a step but with *a step in the right direction*, followed by another and another."

Unfortunately, in today's world of fitness, it's difficult to know what path to follow. Even a very intelligent person, with the best intent, can easily find him or herself arriving at one dead end after another, going around in circles, completely lost. That's the downside of health and fitness misinformation, disinformation, fads, and frauds. And, it's something we must all be cautious of.

So how do you know if you're taking a step in the right direction? How do you have a successful journey from Point A (where you are) to Point B (where you want to be, your destination)? That's a darn good question. One that needs to be answered before we move on to the specific nutrition and exercise components of my ABSolution Program. Answering that question is what this chapter's about. And to do that, I'd like to share with you five very important lessons I've learned about how to experience a successful "fitness journey."

"A successful journey starts not just with a step but with *a step in the right direction*, followed by another and another."

One of the many important lessons I've learned is that you have to know where you're going in order to get there. Makes sense, right? Unfortunately, I'm often reminded that many people overlook this fundamental point. I see them "jump in their car, turn on the engine, and take off," without even knowing where they're going. In no time, they're lost and unmotivated.

If you really want to get "there," first determine where your "there" is. Here's how: start by giving it some thought, then clearly state, in writing, where you want to end before you begin. This is an absolutely essential step in succeeding at anything, especially something as challenging as becoming so fit that you develop your best abs. Keep in mind that your "destination" is your "goal," and you need to be specific not only about where you're going but how much time you're going to give yourself to get there. For example, someone might decide that their destination—their goal—is to weigh 184 lbs with 8% bodyfat and "arrive" with a 32-inch waistline. That's how simple it is. That's a specific destination. Add a "timeline" to that, such as, "I will get 'there' within 12 weeks," and you'll be further along in your journey already than the vast majority of people who endeavor to become more fit.

Here's another important lesson: once you decide where you want to go, you need to become very clear about where you're starting from. You need to identify your "Point A." Keep in mind, if you don't know where you stand, it's hard to know where to step. And it's impossible to follow a map from one point to another if you don't know where you are beginning. That's where self-assessment and evaluation comes in, which can be as simple as taking a before photo and measuring your bodyfat, your scale weight, and your waistline. For example, a man might determine, through these basic measurements, that he weighs 197 lbs with 16% bodyfat and a 36-inch waistline. He could take a "before" photo of himself, attach those "stats" to the photo, and, along the bottom, write, "As of this date (and list a specific date), *I am here*." Then he could attach his determined destination to that, and he will have complete clarity about his Points A and B. Sounds pretty simple, right? Well, it sounds that way because *it is*. It really is simple. But, if you don't do this, you'll find that succeeding at building a better body is downright difficult, if not impossible.

A third lesson I have to share is that after you determine your "Points A and B," you must make sure you select an accurate "map." You must have the right information. You must have a plan, and you must follow that plan. Your plan should be proven; otherwise you will be engaging in "guesswork" or "trial and error," which is not necessary when it comes to fitness. There is a *science* to this. The results you will experience from following a proven plan are predictable and can be replicated.

Without a proven plan, how can you know if you're exercising too much or too little; if you're over- or under-eating; if you're getting the right amount of rest and relaxation, etc.? The answer is... you won't know! My advice: *don't guess!*

Rest assured, the ABSolution Program is an accurate, straightforward map—it is a proven fat-loss and muscle-defining plan. Follow it, and it will help you keep from getting lost and wasting time. That, you'll learn for yourself when you begin to apply the information you'll find throughout this book.

A fourth lesson I've learned is that *progress is made where progress is measured.* In order to have a successful journey, you need to watch for various "signposts" along the way to assure you that you are getting closer and closer to your destination. A simple way to do that is by measuring your bodyfat, scale weight, and waistline as well as taking photos every four weeks so you can actually see you're getting there—that you are a success in progress. For example, if you've decided to lose 17 lbs of bodyfat in 12 weeks, after 4 weeks, you should be able to measure that you've lost about 6 lbs of bodyfat and are well on your way to arriving at your destination on time.

When you do that, not only will your continual progress feed your inspiration and motivation, but you will also find that you're gaining energy and momentum the further along you go because you'll be able to measure that you're getting closer and closer to your destination.

And finally, I've learned that even if you know where you're going, know where you're starting from, have accurate information and a proven plan, and even if you measure your progress along the way, you must stay focused to succeed!

Unfortunately, what often happens is that people begin their journey with laser-like focus and resolve, but along the way, all these interesting "alternative routes" pop up, and they start taking unnecessary detours. What many of these people discover, and one of the things that you might have learned also, is that once you go off course, it's hard to get back on track. You lose your momentum at least and may even get completely lost!

Consider this: the fastest way to get from Point A to Point B is with *a straight line.* That means we need to avoid detours and dead ends and do whatever we can to rise above the clutter (misinformation, myths, fitness frauds, and fads) and fly a direct route toward our destination.

I highly encourage you to have faith in the information in this book and allow it to be your guide—your treasure map—your plan and your path. I encourage you to start with a step in the right direction, followed by another and another. Start strong and finish even *stronger.* Stay focused and do not give up! When you do that, you can make a remarkable transformation in your physique, faster than you might have even believed possible.

CHAPTER **FIVE**

Make It or
Break It

I would be hard pressed to tell you the capitol of South Dakota, explain microeconomics, or tell you what is causing global warming. I can't explain the popularity of professional wrestling, why anyone would eat at Taco Bell, nor the rise and fall of communism. But there is one thing I know with crystal clarity: *it's habits that make us, and it's habits that break us*. And nowhere is that more true than when it comes to nutrition and exercise. How you eat and how you exercise (or don't exercise) determines how you look and feel more than any other aspect of your lifestyle. And to succeed, we have to learn how to nourish good habits while starving the bad ones.

As much as I might like you to believe that my physical condition has to do with super-human willpower, an exceptionally high IQ, or superior genetics, the fact is, I have been able to achieve this level of fitness and maintain it for nearly two decades primarily because of my habits. I'll take credit for that. And having healthy habits is something everyone can enjoy. It isn't unique to me.

Now when I talk about habits, I'm referring to those subconscious things we do day in and day out. The things we do automatically, without even thinking about them. We certainly have habits for how we eat. And we also have habits for how we speak, how we work, how we work out, even for how we drive home from work. When you repeat something again and again, when you train yourself to do something (either intentionally or accidentally), it becomes a habit. Quite simply, good habits are ones that help you move toward your desired objectives. Bad habits are the ones that get in the way.

Unfortunately, as a nation, we have some very unhealthy habits, and we are paying the price: over $100 billion last year alone. A recent report issued by the Surgeon General shows that the number of adolescents who are obese has tripled since 1980, while the number of adults who are obese has doubled. Tragically, *more than 1,000 people a day die from diseases caused by unhealthy habits!* This is becoming a national

"I know with crystal clarity: *it's habits that make us, and it's habits that break us.*"

epidemic; in fact, some experts project that if the situation doesn't change by the year 2025, 75% of all Americans will be clinically obese.

So why is this happening? Is it because Americans don't have the money to eat right? That doesn't add up; America is among the richest nations in the world. Is it because Americans don't have access to healthy foods? That can't be it either; nowhere in the world do people have as much variety of healthy foods to choose from as we do here. Is it because Americans are lazy? That is definitely not the case; America was founded by hard-working, bright, innovative men and women—that's our heritage. So what is the problem? Well, the way I see it, it's that Americans, in general, simply have some very poor fitness habits: eating too much, exercising too little.

Clearly, something needs to change. And that "something" is our habits. So how do we change those habits? Good question. Here's my answer...

Before you jump in and start randomly making changes, make sure you carefully determine what needs to change. Become informed and aware. Then decide to intentionally change the habit from bad to good. Typically, the good habit you need to develop is the opposite of the bad habit holding you back. A simple example: not planning what you'll eat or when you'll eat is a bad habit—it forces you to rely on last-minute decision making and guesswork. The opposite of that is, of course, carefully planning your nutrition ahead of time, which will enable you to make sure that you have healthy, nutritious foods available when and where you need them.

Long-term success relies on changing bad habits into good ones, not merely suppressing unhealthy habits for a period of time until willpower gives out and the unhealthy habits return. That's the problem with quick-fix "diets" and other pseudosolutions like liposuction: they do not require you to change the habits that caused the problem to begin with. Very often, extra fat around your midsection is only one of many symptoms and signs that what you're doing—your habits—*are not working for you.*

One of the reasons that Bill's Body-*for*-LIFE Program has worked, long term, for so many thousands of people is because at its core, it is a habit-transforming program. To follow it, a person has to change numerous habits. When they do, their bodies are changed, and their health improves, for life.

Developing a new habit is always hard before it's easy. For example, the first month or so of beginning to exercise intensely first thing in the morning requires diligent, conscious effort. It's work! However, the good news is that it does not take extraordinary willpower to maintain healthy habits. Once you develop new habits, you will do them just as automatically as any other habit. You will reach for a nutrition shake just as "naturally" as you may have reached for a cheeseburger.

As we move on to the specific nutrition and exercise information, I will teach you the habits that form my lifestyle, and I encourage you to carefully examine my habits, compare them to your own, and look for areas where you can improve. When you embrace the nutrition and exercise habits I will share with you in the following chapters, you will be able to lose fat and sculpt a lean, muscular midsection. And, like me, you will be able to maintain that condition as long as you so desire.

CHAPTER SIX

Nourishing
Your Success

My approach to nutrition is a balance between good old fashioned common sense and modern science. That has been my approach for the past 20 years, and it will be my approach for the next 20. Unfortunately, most people don't take that approach. They fall for one fad after another—trying diets that are ineffective, unproven, and in some cases, extremely unhealthy. It's no wonder people often give up hope of ever understanding nutrition well enough to get in great shape. But it doesn't have to be that way! Virtually all of us are capable of learning how to feed our bodies properly and enjoy the benefits of doing so.

My objective is not to try to impress you by presenting you with page after page of scientific facts about nutrition, proteins, carbohydrates, and the chemistry of how vitamins and minerals work within our bodies. That information is available in virtually any college textbook, and it's certainly something you can access in a few minutes on the internet. I want to give you something more useful than that. I want to give you some insight into what I really do.

All you really need to know to understand my nutrition program is included in this chapter. I'll first share with you information about the basics—teaching you precisely which foods and how much of them you will need to maximize the results you experience from the ABSolution workout, which we'll get into in the next chapter. I'll also give you some insight into modern advances in nutritional science that will help you get even better results faster.

Let's start with the fundamentals: food plays a prominent role in the development of every cell in our bodies (and there are trillions of them). That's where the popular saying "you are what you eat" originates. These nutrients include proteins, carbohydrates, fats, vitamins, minerals, and water. The key is learning how much of these nutrients you need to eat and when to eat them to feed your muscles and starve the fat.

Protein is the cornerstone of each of my meals. Here are a few things about protein that are important to understand: first of all, as you may very well know, high-quality protein comes from foods like chicken, fish, beef, egg whites, soy beans, and some dairy products (like cottage cheese). And, there are also a variety of protein supplements on the market; my favorite is high-quality whey protein. All of these foods offer quality sources of complete proteins. It's important to note that complete proteins contain all the essential amino acids. (They're essential because your body can't make them on its own, so they must be provided through the foods we eat.) Those amino acids are the basic building blocks of muscle as well as a countless number of enzymes, hormones, neurotransmitters, and antibodies. Amino acids flow through the bloodstream and are delivered to systems in our bodies that depend on them. *Protein is a very, very important nutrient*, especially for people who are trying to build leaner, stronger, healthier bodies because exercise increases the body's "turnover rate" of amino acids, thereby increasing daily requirements.

Carbohydrates are vitally important to your health as well. Found in fruits, vegetables, grains, pasta, bread, and cereal, carbohydrates are the primary source of energy your body derives "blood sugar" or glucose from. Carbohydrates trigger the release of insulin, a powerful hormone needed to help amino acids enter muscle cells, which is very important. In that way, carbohydrates and protein work together, which is why I include both in almost every meal.

There are two basic types of carbohydrates: simple and complex. Generally, I eat complex carbohydrates: my favorite sources are brown rice, sweet potatoes/yams, vegetables, oatmeal, and whole-grain pasta. These complex or "slow carbs" provide the body with a consistent release of energy and help you feel good and healthy.

Simple carbohydrates pack more of a punch—they are quickly converted to blood sugar after you eat them. Refined sugar, most fruits and fruit juices, and white breads and pastas are sources of simple carbohydrates. They cause your blood sugar to rise rapidly, which signals the rapid release of insulin as well, which shuttles the glucose into muscle, the liver, or fat cells. Now, if you need instant energy, for example if you're going for a run, hiking, skiing, playing football or basketball, and your endurance is fading, that's when consuming a simple carbohydrate performance drink like Gatorade or a Power Bar can be a good thing. Those quick carbs can keep you going strong but not for long.

In terms of fat loss, simple carbohydrates are not a good thing; because of the powerful and sudden effect they have, they can interfere with fat loss and also cause a spike in energy and then a sudden crash. When the latter occurs, you will often feel very hungry—that's the body demanding more blood sugar—demanding more food. I avoid this problem by choosing primarily complex carbohydrate foods (although I usually have one piece of fruit each day), and I combine my carbs with protein, which helps make the energy release even more stable.

The next nutrient that's important to have a basic understanding of is fat. Despite the widely held belief that to be healthy you need to completely eliminate fat from your diet, *you actually do need some fat* in the form of essential fatty acids. Knowing which type of fat is good for you and which type is bad is not complicated. Saturated fats are the bad ones. They don't play any important role in the body except to be burned as a back-up form of fuel. Quite simply, you don't need saturated fats at all, but the typical American diet is rich in saturated fats—it's what's in cheeseburgers, French fries, chips, donuts, candy bars, nachos, etc. Saturated fat is solid at room temperature (like butter), and it's the fat that can cause heart disease, cancer, type 2 diabetes, and, of course, can cause you to gain bodyfat. So, I consume very little saturated fat and recommend you limit consumption as well.

Unsaturated fats are usually liquid at room temperature—they are the healthier fats. Specific unsaturated fats cannot be made by the body and are necessary for thousands of biochemical reactions—these are known as essential fatty acids. Essential fatty acids include linolenic acid and linoleic acid, or as scientists often refer to them, omega-3 and omega-6

fatty acids. They must be provided from the foods you eat—your body can't make them on its own. And, without these fatty acids, you will not be able to maximize your body's ability to burn stored bodyfat. A deficiency of essential fatty acids will interfere with the optimal function of each and every cell in your body as its outer layer, or cell membrane, is comprised primarily of essential fats. Very often, when people clean up their diets and start eating only low-fat foods, they notice their skin and hair become unhealthy, and their energy levels fall dramatically; some people even get dizzy or light-headed. These can be signs of a deficiency of essential fatty acids.

Cold-water fish (which have a higher fat content than warm-water fish), such as salmon, mackerel, and trout, have linolenic acid (omega-3) in them. Low-fat fish like haddock, sole, and flounder contain almost insignificant amounts of these important fatty acids. (Shellfish are generally not a good source, either.) Now, you can either eat a lot of fish, or you can make sure you eat oils high in fatty acids. Good sources of linoleic acid (omega-6) include canola oil, safflower oil, sunflower oil, and soybean oil. But, above all else, I feel the best source of essential fatty acids is flaxseed oil, which I eat one tablespoon of every day. I add it to my nutrition shakes or put it on a salad or rice. Flaxseed oil tastes good, and you can get it at virtually any health-food store.

All three of the nutrients I've talked about so far—proteins, carbohydrates, and essential fatty acids—need to be consumed daily in relatively significant quantities that are measured in ounces or grams. Scientists call these "macronutrients" (macro meaning large). The other essential nutrients I'm going to tell you about now are consumed in very small quantities (often measured in milligrams); they're known as the "micronutrients" (micro meaning small). These are the vitamins and minerals. Although only small amounts of these nutrients are needed by the body, they play a vital role in maintaining the proper biological functioning of everything from your muscles to your mind. Vitamins and minerals contribute to good health, muscle growth, and proper fat burning by regulating the metabolism and assisting the biochemical processes that release energy from the food you eat. If you don't take in enough of these essential micronutrients to maintain proper levels, deficiency symptoms, which include muscle weakness, slow fat loss, connective-tissue deterioration, and frequent colds and infections due to suppression of the immune system, just to name a few, will appear.

Vitamins are "organic" compounds, which means they are produced naturally in both vegetables and animals, where they are found in abundant quantities. The main function of vitamins in the body are to help enzymes with reactions, including energy metabolism, protein synthesis, nutrient digestion and absorption, to name but a few of thousands. Vitamins are essential—*you cannot live without them.* Literally.

Vitamins are either fat soluble or water soluble, depending on whether fat- or water-based molecules transport the vitamin through the bloodstream. Fat-soluble vitamins include A, D, E, and K. Because these vitamins have an affinity for fat, they can be stored in both adipose (fat) tissue and in the liver, extending their functional life span in the body and strongly decreasing the chance of developing deficiencies. The water-soluble vitamins include all of the B vitamins and Vitamin C; they aren't stored in the body for more than a few hours, so daily intake is a must.

Minerals are inorganic in nature, meaning they are not produced by plants nor animals. They can, however, be found in food sources, for example, iron in red meat, calcium in milk, and potassium in bananas. Minerals are extremely important for your body to work right. They are essential for nerve cell communication, flexing muscles, fluid balance, and energy production. Many minerals also serve as building blocks for body tissues, such as calcium and phosphorus for bones.

Minerals are referred to as either "bulk" or "trace" depending on the amount needed by the body. Bulk minerals include calcium, magnesium, phosphorous, potassium, and sodium. Trace minerals, on the other hand, may be required in quantities as little as a few micrograms (that's one one-thousandth of a milligram). These include chromium, cobalt, copper, iron, selenium, silicon, and zinc.

Now, I need to tell you a few things about water. Water is not a nutrient by definition, but it's so important to good health—it is absolutely *essential* for building and maintaining your best body. Water covers approximately 70% of the earth's surface and makes up about 70% of our bodies as well. *All living things rely on water to thrive, you and I included.* It helps produce energy, detoxify our bodies, regulate body temperature, build new cells, and lubricate joints, among thousands of other functions.

We naturally lose water every minute of every day, just through breathing. During the summer months, water losses are greater because perspiration, which is used to cool our bodies, evaporates faster in a hot environment. Caffeinated and alcoholic beverages are diuretics—they cause you to lose even more body water. Water losses of a mere *one percent* of your bodyweight can impair functioning both *mentally and physically!* Losses of four percent can cause headaches, loss of energy, muscle weakness, and irritability. Losses of seven percent can be fatal.

Don't wait until you're thirsty to drink water, or you'll put back less than what you really need. It is essential that you replenish your water losses daily. It's not a discussion topic for good company, but watching your urine may be the best way to tell if your body's properly hydrated. Dark, gold-colored urine is a sure sign that you're low on fluids. Drink enough water to aim for light-yellow or, better yet, almost clear urine. The average person needs at least 10 cups of water per day. People who exercise regularly need even more. I drink water from dawn to dusk, and then some. I drink 16 ounces of bottled or filtered water first thing in the morning and another 16 ounces during my workouts. All total, I drink a gallon of water each and every day, and I drink an extra cup of water for each cup of coffee or diet soda I drink during the day. I suggest you do the same.

Now, I want to share some important information with you about nutritional supplements. There are so many questions people have about supplements and a great deal of confusion in this area of nutrition as well. I believe that at best, supplements offer a nutritional advantage that can improve the results you experience from a good exercise program and may also extend and improve the quality of your life. At worst, I believe supplements are the fitness industry's most embarrassing fraud *(although the infomercial ab-exercise gadgets are closing in fast)!* On one end of the spectrum, you have legitimate, state-of-the-art, scientifically developed and tested dietary supplements that exert powerful and beneficial effects on health and performance. On the other end of the spectrum, you have worthless, sometimes even dangerous "miracle pills" and potions being peddled by hucksters who are nothing more than snake-oil salesmen. The hard part for many people is determining which is which. It's hard to know who and what to believe. It's hard to know what really works, and it's important to determine what's right for you.

Here are a few things about choosing nutritional supplements that you can absolutely, positively count on: first, *virtually every adult in America can benefit, to some degree, by supplementing with vitamins and minerals daily.* Most scientists and medical doctors agree with me on that. Even people who try to eat healthy can't always be sure that the foods they're eating were grown in soil that isn't "farmed out" and depleted of minerals, nor can they be sure that the fresh-looking fruits and vegetables from their local market are really fresh and still rich with nutrients. Simply consuming a quality multivitamin and mineral supplement in the form of a capsule or having at least one nutrition shake, fortified with vitamins and minerals, each day can make a big difference. I do both—I take a multivitamin and mineral supplement, and I also drink at least one Myoplex nutrition shake each day. I think of Myoplex as high-tech, healthy fast food and have used it for over five years now. It is especially helpful when I travel and don't have access to my own kitchen. Beyond supplementing the very basics, some people, especially those who are pushing themselves very hard during their workouts, may very well benefit from taking other scientifically developed and tested nutritional supplements. Ones I use daily include *creatine* and *7-Keto.*

If you would like more information about supplements, please visit www.Nutros.com which is an online, interactive supplement guide that I've developed to help people understand exactly how they can benefit from the latest scientific breakthroughs in nutritional science. Nutros.com is a website I've been working on for years. It is now one of the world's largest nutrition and vitamin research libraries. You simply visit the website, answer a few questions about what your health and fitness goals are, and the interactive Nutros.com Personal Solutions Builder guides you through a course in how you can get better results faster with the intelligent, common sense use of nutritional supplements. At Nutros.com, you can also compare the prices and ingredients of different brands of supplements. This *helps save you time and money* and helps make sure you don't get ripped off.

A few final words on supplements: follow your instincts/intuition. And use your mind before you reach into your pocket and shell out hard-earned money for supplements that are marketed as miracles in a bottle. Even the best supplements are merely an extra edge and only work if you're consuming healthy whole foods, drinking plenty of water, and exercising regularly. I realize you already know that—I'm just reminding you.

Another topic I want to address is the popular fad diets that ask you to eat low or no carbs. I've evaluated dozens and dozens of different types of diets and nutrition programs over the years, and I have discovered *absolutely nothing works better than balancing proteins, carbohydrates, and essential fatty acids with ample amounts of water, vitamins, and minerals.* I believe all of these nutrients exist in nature and have been a part of the human diet for eons for a very good reason—because *they are good for you!* That's why I don't believe in the popular low-carb diets or any other nutrition program that is not a balanced approach.

It's vitally important to learn both what to eat, as well as how much to feed your body to achieve the results you desire. In America today, the habit is to consume too much—portion sizes are out of control, and as the food industry continues to "super size" portions, people are eating more and more. The cause and effect is obvious. As portions sizes are going up, so is the percentage of American adults and children who are being "super sized." I don't want that to happen to you, but it will if you eat too much and don't control your portion sizes.

Now, in order to determine how much food you need, you don't have to count calories or weigh your food. Personally, I've found calorie counting to be very ineffective, impractical, and unreliable. Instead of counting calories or weighing my food, I've literally learned to measure the proper portions of food for me by sight. I can look at a plate of food and tell you if it's too much, too little, or if it's perfectly balanced. And, you can learn this as well. And when you do, you will find that it is a lot more effective and a lot more practical than counting calories.

One way to control portion sizes is to *use smaller plates* than most people. A dinner plate that is no more than eight inches in diameter is about right for most men, and for women, a six-inch plate will do. Divide the plate, with imaginary lines, into thirds. Then, fill up a third of the plate with a lean, quality source of protein like broiled salmon or chicken; fill up a third of the plate with a healthy complex carbohydrate such as steamed brown rice, whole grain pasta, or a sweet potato; and fill up another third of the plate with a fresh, steamed vegetable, like broccoli, carrots, or green beans. When my plate is full, I know the portions are right for me. And I don't eat any more than that. I don't need any more than that in one meal, and you don't either.

If you eat too much at once, not only will you not be able to properly digest it all (which is why so many people suffer from indigestion!) but you also won't be hungry again in just a few hours, which is when you need to eat again.

I consume balanced, portion-controlled meals every two to three hours, for a total of six daily meals. I eat a lot of protein in the form of egg whites, fish, chicken, and non-fat cottage cheese. I combine that with complex carbohydrates like brown rice, yams, or whole-grain pasta. I consume a nutrition shake when I don't have time for a healthy meal. And I take my supplements. I do this day in and day out. In Chapter Eleven, I give you more examples of how I eat to build muscle and lose fat.

Remember that you can't eat right unless you stock your kitchen with healthy, nourishing food. Be careful to buy only foods at the grocery store that

> **"The key is learning how to consume the right amount of each essential nutrient at just the right time."**

will nourish your success. Do not buy junk food, and if you have it in your home now, *please* get rid of it.

Just as important as knowing what to eat is understanding what not to eat. Here's where I encourage you to rely on a healthy serving of good old-fashioned common sense. You know darn well that you can't put a cheeseburger in your mouth and not expect to see it on your belly. You know that to get in extraordinarily good condition—to get your bodyfat down so low that you can see sharp definition in your abdominal muscles, you absolutely, positively *cannot* regularly eat French fries, pizza, donuts, cookies, ice cream, Big Mac's, fried chicken, nachos, and so on. Junk food, fast food, candy, cakes... You know you're going to have to avoid these types of food to be successful on the ABSolution Program. If you have a habit of eating any of these foods, let me assure you, you can switch that behavior, with conscious effort and practice. If you crave these types of foods, please realize it's not because your body needs them, it's because that's been your habit. In time, you can literally kill cravings for almost any junk food by replacing the unhealthy foods you used to eat with healthy and satisfying alternatives. I crave fish, brown rice, and vegetables the same way other people crave nachos and beer.

Once again, I cannot emphasize enough that the key to eating right is learning how to consume the right foods that contain essential nutrients, at the right times. Then, you need to make this way of eating a habit by doing it day after day for at least a month. After that, it will feel right, and you will follow it naturally. And *you will enjoy the results!* This is a smart, safe, and practical approach that will nourish your success, as it has mine.

CHAPTER SEVEN

Exercising
Common Sense

I am very often asked, "Shawn, which exercises do you do for your abs?" My answer is, *"All of them!"* Squats, leg presses, biceps curls, shoulder presses, bench presses, sprinting, stair climbing... *every* exercise I do helps me sculpt a lean, muscular midsection. It's not just the crunches, the leg lifts, and the other direct abdominal exercises that build and define the abs. But most people I've met have fallen for the myth that to build great abs, you simply need to do sit-ups or some other ab exercise for a few minutes each day. There are literally millions of people out there who have tried that approach. They bought the ab-exercise devices. They followed the instructions and have gotten *absolutely nowhere.*

Rest assured, the ABSolution Program is different. It's based on the scientifically sound but often overlooked approach that the best "fat-burning exercise" you could possibly do is *building muscle.* It's a fact: nothing burns fat better than healthy muscles!

You see, in my body and yours, there are over 600 muscles made up of over a billion muscle fibers. A healthy human body is made up of over half muscle. And muscle doesn't just sit there looking good; it controls the metabolic rate, it's literally the armor that protects us, it allows us to walk, run, work, and play. It allows us to live and enjoy life. However, when our muscles are not properly cared for, they deteriorate. When that happens, we gain fat, and we become weak and vulnerable to injury. Health begins to fail. Vitality fades.

So how do we properly care for our muscles? Well, as I'm certain you are aware, regular physical activity and exercise is essential. However, the latest statistics show that eight out of ten people in America don't do enough exercise to keep their muscles in shape. That's one of those bad habits of modern life. We've invented machines to do so much of the physical work that our parents and grandparents used to have to do. And, virtually every day, more inventions—more machines—more motors and computers are making the sedentary life an option for more people.

All of this makes it even that much more important to follow a *smart* exercise program—an exercise program that includes both aerobics and strength training. I believe *a balanced approach* to exercise is the way to go, just as I believe that a balanced approach to nutrition is the best strategy. I do not favor exercise programs that include only weight lifting, and I do not recommend a routine that includes only aerobics. Both offer substantial benefits, and both forms of exercise complement each other and enhance your ability to burn bodyfat and build strong, healthy muscles.

Another thing about exercise I want to point out is that during our workouts, we're trying to *prime* the muscles, *not* pulverize them. I've discovered that short, highly intense workouts are the most efficient and effective. It's *quality* not quantity that matters when it comes to exercise. It's *focused intensity* and giving each and every rep of each and every set your best effort and then some.

The fundamental scientific principle at the foundation of my program is that for a muscle to become stronger, healthier, and more efficient at burning fat, it has to be stressed beyond the point that it is accustomed to. Only then will it adapt. Scientists call this "progressive resistance exercise." What that means is that the exercise intensity or quality needs to consistently increase over time. Otherwise, the time and effort you spend exercising doesn't really pay off. And this is the reason a lot of people get stuck at plateaus and have difficulty getting in better shape—they're simply not working out hard enough. Sure, they might be in the gym for two hours each day, but the amount of time is *not* the only factor that determines the effectiveness of your workouts. It's the focused intensity that counts!

So, what happens if you combine time and effort? What happens if you work out really hard, for a really long time? Well, that's not the right approach either. Your body can recover from only a certain amount of intense training. If you go past that point, a point that some people call "overtraining," you actually go backward instead of forward—you actually *lose* muscle size and strength.

Another consequence of overtraining that is often overlooked is that it can become a form of emotional stress that is very uncomfortable. When people are uncomfortable, their instincts drive them to do things that make them feel comfortable. One of these behaviors is eating "comfort foods," which are generally high-carbohydrate foods, like ice cream, donuts, pizza, etc. Also, when you increase your level of stress too much, your body releases extra amounts of a hormone called cortisol, which has been shown in scientific studies to slow the fat-burning process and also increase the amount of fat stored in the belly. I can't emphasize this point enough: the right amount of intense exercise makes you feel good and helps you look good. It increases your energy. But too much has the opposite effect.

Now it's very important to understand what I mentioned earlier about priming the muscle, not pulverizing it. The way to build stronger, healthier muscles is to *work out intensely and then allow the body to rest and recover* while you feed it with the nutrients it needs. This approach is what I call "exercising common sense."

Unfortunately, when it comes to ab training, more than any other muscle group, people engage in a type of training that absolutely makes no sense: they do low-intensity, high-rep workouts too often. This training method is fueled by the myth that you can spot reduce fat from the belly. The fact is you can't. High-repetition sets of crunches and sit-ups performed frequently don't stimulate muscle development nor burn enough fat to alter your waistline.

You see, the body's fat cells, whether they are in your belly, buns, lower back, or the cheeks on your face, "stick together." You can't lose fat off your belly without losing fat everywhere else on your body. I know sometimes that's hard to believe because these "problem areas" (the belly for men and typically the hips for women) are so conspicuous and frustrating that they distort our perspective. The fact is, when we're gaining fat, we're gaining it all over—we're gaining it wherever fat is stored. And, when we are losing fat, we're losing it all over. So *please* don't waste your time trying to "spot reduce" problem areas. It flat out doesn't work!

The way to decrease your overall bodyfat percentage and reveal your abs is by eating right, as we discussed in the last chapter, and following an

exercise program that helps you build muscle—one that includes weight-training exercises for the entire body, combined with just the right amount of cardio.

That's how you burn bodyfat, but if you want abs like mine, you've got to build the muscles of the midsection as well. And to do that, *you have to train the abs like you would the biceps, triceps, quadriceps, and deltoids.* Can you imagine finishing a leg workout and then picking up a couple five-pound dumbbells and doing a hundred reps of curls because you want lean, sculpted biceps? You probably wouldn't do that because you probably know it wouldn't work. Well, unfortunately, many people just don't know that kind of approach to ab training just doesn't work. Here's why: the abdominal muscles are made up of primarily fast-twitch muscle fibers, just like the other major muscles I mentioned above. Those types of muscle fibers respond to high-intensity, relatively low-rep training.

I train my abs two or three times a week at the most. I perform basic but effective exercises, and I focus very intensely during my workouts. In the next chapter, I'll show you my favorite exercises, and you will notice that I emphasize the proper form because I believe you can't have "exercise quality" without doing the right exercises the right way. This helps you stimulate the development of sculpted abdominal muscles and ensures that you'll be able to do these exercises safely, which is essential for long-term success. Please be sure to follow my advice about how to do these exercises carefully. You'll get better results faster and be able to

"The way to decrease your overall bodyfat percentage and reveal your abs is by eating right and following an exercise program that helps you build muscle."

lower your risk of injury, which, unfortunately, is something many people are unnecessarily experiencing as they head for the gym loaded with ambition but devoid of proper instruction.

As you'll discover in the following chapters, I not only train my abdominal muscles with high-intensity exercises, *I train every major muscle group of the body with high-intensity resistance exercise.* By developing the complete muscle structure of the body, literally from head to toe, you not only build a truly classic, heroic, proportional physique, you also build functional strength. You build the type of body that will help you enjoy recreational sports like I enjoy, such as snowboarding, mountain biking, hiking, etc. That's another one of the benefits of the ABSolution Program which you can't enjoy if you follow an unsafe, unsound program which just emphasizes your abs. Another danger of just training abs and not training your other muscles is suffering a lower back injury, something millions of Americans experienced last year and had to take time off of work. They couldn't continue their exercise programs, and oftentimes couldn't even go for a walk.

Training safely is a part of ensuring training consistency, and another component of consistency is making daily exercise a part of your lifestyle. I think *the best time of day to exercise is the time when you will actually make it a habit.* Statistics show that people who begin an exercise program and exercise first thing in the morning are three times more likely to stick with it for at least three months. So if you've had trouble being consistant with your workouts in the past, consider training in the morning. I enjoy starting my day with aerobic exercise, and I enjoy doing my weight-training routine in the evening, as it helps me relax and wind down from a hectic day at work. But that's my habit.

Aside from exercising at the time of day when it will work with your schedule, it's important to remember that your exercise program should be coordinated with your nutrition program. Scientific research shows that if you eat right before your workout, you burn less fat. And, aerobic exercise, performed in the morning on an empty stomach, may burn up to three times more fat than the same amount of exercise in the evening, after you've eaten several meals. Some scientists and physiologists debate this, but I personally have seen a greater fat-burning effect from aerobic exercise if I do it in the morning before I eat. And, I actually find that I'm stronger and get a better weight-lifting workout if I do it in the early evening, around six or seven o'clock, which is after I've had four nutritious meals. However, I try not to eat for a few hours before my weight-training workouts, as it has also been shown that certain anabolic hormones, like testosterone and growth hormone, are activated by exercising on an empty stomach as well. By the way, these hormones play an important role in muscle recovery.

Once you make exercise a part of your lifestyle, it will feel more natural to do it than to not do it. You must commit yourself. And at first you must push yourself to do something that doesn't feel natural or comfortable. I encourage you to give it time. Learn to recognize that every time you complete an exercise session, you've taken another step in the right direction. Every time you get up and go to the gym and work out hard when your old habit might have been sitting down and watching TV, you've taken another step in the right direction. Take it one day at a time, and *you will get there!*

Learn to recognize that although working out may not feel good—in fact, an intense workout may actually be downright uncomfortable—in the long run, you're going to feel good—you're going to feel better than ever before. My experience has been that *the harder you push yourself, the better it feels when you're done.* Don't expect it to be easy. And remember that this is one thing no one can do for you. You and you alone are the one who has to do that exercise, who has to get up out of bed early, get on that StairMaster or treadmill and not just "get it over with" but focus on it and give it your very best effort. You and you alone must put your hands around those dumbbells, grip them with all your might, and lift them, again and again, until your muscles burn and then literally give out. Make no mistake, *it takes a strong mind to build a strong body!* And, as you're discovering, success is more a matter of exercising common sense than most people have been led to believe.

CHAPTER EIGHT

My ABSolute
Favorites

Despite the fact that millions of ab-training gadgets, exercise devices, and videos have been sold over the last few years alone, you'll find very few people who can lift up their shirts and actually show you a "six pack." However, what I've discovered is that while these same people are capable of building definition in their abdominals, they're going about it the wrong way! In fact, most people don't even know what the ab muscles really are. And as I eluded to in the last chapter, most people aren't training them properly, much less following a complete approach like the ABSolution Program, which addresses fat loss *and* developing the muscles.

What I will do in this chapter is teach you a little about anatomy and physiology, sharing information about what the abs are and how they function. Then I'll guide you through my absolute favorite ab exercises. They're safe, they're effective, and they will help you sculpt and define all the muscles of the midsection. These are the exercises I include in my own workouts. And, not to brag, but at 38 years of age, my abs are in better shape now than ever.

I'll start with an overview of the abdominal muscles. I see the muscles of the abs as divided into three regions, each of which I recommend you train in each session. As we move forward in this chapter and go through the step-by-step instructions for each of the ab exercises I recommend, notice I've indicated which of the three primary regions each ab exercise works. I've done this so you can be sure to include an exercise for each of the three main areas in every ab workout. When you train each region, you'll be developing the entire midsection, sculpting that chiseled, narrow, and defined look!

Most people are not aware of the fact that they need to do exercises for all three of these regions. They often focus primarily on only the upper region of the abs and then wonder why they're not getting results. What you're going to learn in this chapter is how to avoid that pitfall and maximize your genetic potential—*to build your own best abs.* Please pay close attention as I present the information in this chapter—it is *very* specific and important.

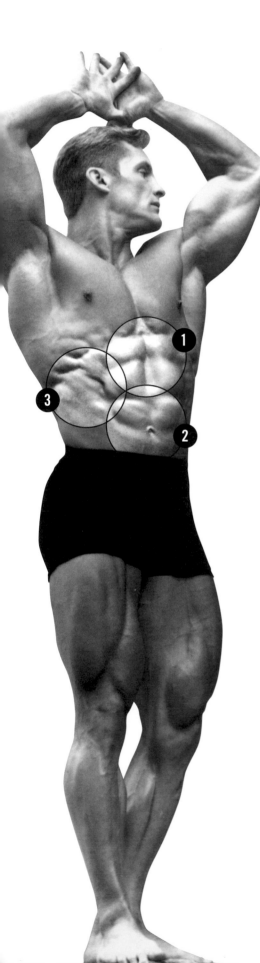

Region 1 is the upper area of the *rectus abdominis*, which is a large muscle that extends across your belly from the rib cage down to your hips. The six-pack look is the result of strong "bands" of connective tissue that form "tendinous intersections" that cut into the rectus abdominis muscle. The more developed the rectus abdominis muscle, the deeper the transverse grooves.

Region 1 is primarily activated during exercises that lift the shoulders from the floor, curling your upper body toward your hips. This includes all types of crunches. To contract the upper abs, simply lean forward and flex. Focus on the muscle region between your rib cage and belly button. When trained intensely, it feels as forceful as contracting or flexing your biceps. Something to be considered when training your abs is that the upper ab region is activated, to some degree, in all ab exercises.

Region 2 of the abs is a continuum of the rectus abdominis found in Region 1. While it is technically one muscle, the regions are isolated by different exercises, placing a very different emphasis on this large muscle. When you are doing an exercise that focuses on Region 2, it will feel much different than the Region 1 exercises.

The lower ab area, or Region 2, is primarily activated during exercises such as leg lifts and reverse crunches where the hips are lifted and rotated upward and inward. The lower abs will fatigue more quickly than the upper abs, at which point, if the exercise is continued, the hip-flexor muscles will take over. When this occurs, you may feel strain in your lower back.

Region 3 is the area of muscles on the sides of the waist, the *oblique* muscles (external and internal rotating obliques). When well developed, they literally frame the abs—an essential part of a great midsection.

The obliques, or Region 3, help you turn from side to side. They're activated by exercises where the upper body is rotated, so it is not aligned with the lower body. They help with twisting the torso and are used heavily in sports that require you to rotate the upper body, such as golf. Exercises that focus on obliques include crossing movements and exercises that require focus on each side separately.

Basic Crunch

Overview

The basic ab crunch is, well… basic. However, it can be an extraordinarily challenging exercise if you perform it with focused intensity! One of the great things about the exercise is that you can do it virtually any time, anywhere. You don't need any equipment, just a floor.

One of the most important things to remember on this exercise is that you should go very slowly. It takes me about two seconds to go from the beginning position of this exercise to the fully contracted position, breathing out slowly on the way up. Once I'm in the contracted position, I continue to flex my abs as hard as I can for a full count of two: "one-thousand-one, one-thousand-two." Then, I slowly return to the starting position while still flexing my abs on the way down. I then relax for a second, take a deep breath in, and repeat.

If you work out at a public gym, you may see people doing variations of this exercise that are all wrong. Some do a full sit-up, where they bring their elbows to their knees. That's not the best way to work your abs, and it's actually one way many people injure their backs. Also, if you watch other people try to perform the crunch, you may notice their feet often come off the floor, their hands are locked behind their heads, and they're pulling their necks too far forward as they try to sit up. That's ineffective and dangerous.

Often times, people do this exercise so fast that they can pump out 50 reps before I've even completed 15. But I can guarantee I get more ab work than they do by following the proper form and focusing intensely on each rep!

Start/Finish

Midpoint

How It's Done

Start by lying on your back with your knees bent and feet resting flat on the floor. Gently position your hands behind your head to support it, not to pull on it. Please do not lock your hands behind your head! You might find it comfortable to lie on a towel or an exercise mat.

Focus your mind on contracting the abdominal muscles before you even begin to lift your shoulders up off the floor. This is very important. We're using the mind to focus the intensity of the exercise.

Contracting the abdominal muscles, curl the shoulders up and forward until the upper back starts to lift off the floor. Do not try to sit all the way up! *Concentrate on flexing the abdominal muscles* when you are lifting the shoulders up, imagining you're trying to make a dent in the floor with your lower back, and let that contraction pull your shoulders off the ground. Hold the contracted position for a full two seconds before slowly returning to the starting position. Then simply repeat.

Training Tip

To increase the range of motion and to get even more ab work, try putting a rolled-up towel under your lower back.

Hip Up

How It's Done

Begin by lying on your back, placing your hands right at the sides of your hips, palms down, with your head resting gently on the floor and your legs pointed straight up at a 90° angle, perpendicular to the floor. Your legs should be straight, but your knees should not be completely locked.

Keeping your legs straight and your feet together, begin to contract your lower abdominal muscles while you breathe out, and slowly roll your hips toward your chest. Slowly lift the hips not just upward but forward while you continue to flex your abs. As soon as your lower back is off the ground and your feet are over your head, pause for a moment and *contract your lower abs* for a full count of two seconds! Then breathe in as you slowly begin to lower your hips back to the floor until you return to the starting position. Take a deep breath, and repeat the exercise.

Start/Finish

Midpoint

Training Tip

It is not necessary to lower the legs past the point where they are perpendicular to the floor. This will not increase the effectiveness of this exercise, and it may cause unnecessary stress and strain to the lower back!

Overview

This relatively basic but challenging floor exercise works Region 2, the lower abs. It's one of the many very effective ab exercises you can do without any equipment at your home or for people who, like myself, travel pretty often, in a hotel room.

Far too often, I see people making the mistake of lowering the legs all the way down to the floor and then swinging them back up above their heads. Not only does this *not* work the abdominal muscles, it can strain the lower back! The proper range of motion in this, like many ab exercises, is relatively short.

I cannot emphasize enough that for the hip up to be an effective ab exercise, it must be done very, very slowly—I take a full two seconds to lift my hips from the starting position to the finish, I hold it in the contracted position for two seconds, and then I lower my hips very slowly, taking another two seconds.

Another mistake people make on this exercise is that they try adding ankle weights or, worse yet, they try to hold a dumbbell between their feet. Please do not make this mistake! That is so dangerous! What good are great abs if you've got a broken nose and scar on your forehead which reads, "York Barbell Company"?!

Focus intensely and go slowly, and this exercise will be plenty intense enough and is a good exercise to help flatten and define the area of your midsection below the belly button.

Side Crunch

Start/Finish

Midpoint

How It's Done

Begin by lying down on the floor with your knees bent and your torso twisted so your left leg is lying flat on the floor but your upper body is still facing upward. Place your hands gently on the sides of your head.

Now, take a deep breath and begin contracting your abdominal muscles. Let that contraction slowly lift your upper body off the floor while you breath out. As soon as your shoulders come slightly off the floor, try to hold that contracted position for a full count of "one-thousand-one, one-thousand-two." Then slowly lower yourself back to the starting position. Perform 12 to 15 repetitions in this position, and then reverse the position so your right leg is touching the floor and perform 12 to 15 more repetitions.

Training Tip

When you rotate your legs to the left, do not allow your upper body to rotate along with it. Keep your shoulders facing upwards.

Overview

This exercise helps to firm and develop the muscles of Region 3, the obliques or sides of the midsection. It requires no exercise equipment and can be done virtually any time, anywhere.

When performing this exercise, it's very important not to pull your head so far forward that your chin touches your chest, as this can put a lot of unnecessary strain on your neck muscles. Also important to completing this exercise with proper form is to keep your upper body facing upward, even though your lower body will be twisted.

As with most of the crunch exercises, the range of motion is very short, which is why it's vitally important to develop the habit of beginning to *contract the abdominal muscles before you even start to lift your shoulders off the ground.* Most people I've met do not take this approach—they quickly rock back and forth, carelessly, without any focus or intensity. Oftentimes, you can hear them at the gym, counting, "One-two-three-four... I can't wait to get these over and get out the door!" Seriously, far too many people have developed the habit of just "pumping out" a certain number of reps and sets on abdominal exercises, and they don't get anything out of the exercise.

My advice is to take your time. Think about the muscle you're training. Go slow and flex, flex, flex!

Reverse Crunch

How It's Done

Begin by lying on your back, knees bent, and feet together, about six inches above the floor. Put your hands behind your head, like you would if you were getting ready to do an ab crunch.

Keeping your feet close to your hips, contract your abs while you slowly *curl your lower body up toward your shoulders,* gradually rolling your hips off the floor. Exhale when you contract the abs, so your rib cage will drop and allow for a more intense muscle contraction. Keep flexing the abs until your hips and lower back are just slightly off the floor. Hold that position for a count of two, and flex as hard as you can! Then slowly lower your hips back to the starting position, take a breath, and repeat. Keep in mind that the slower you do this exercise, the better it works.

Start/Finish

Midpoint

Training Tip

One variation of this exercise I often perform simply involves placing the hands, palms down, by your hips. This is a bit harder and more intense.

Overview

This is a relatively basic exercise that works Region 2, the lower abs. It does not require any exercise equipment to perform, which makes it great for home workouts.

Remember that the abdominal muscles are responsible for shortening the distance between your hips and your shoulders. You can do that by either lifting the hips and bringing them up, which is what we're doing in this exercise, or you can lift the upper body and bring it toward the hips, which is what we do in the standard crunch. Also, remember that we must include exercises for the lower region as well as the upper region. If we don't, we'll never get that flat, defined look below the belly button, which very few people achieve.

It may take a while to get to the point where you can do this exercise effectively, because oftentimes the muscles in Region 2 are a bit "rusty." Basically, what that means is that the "neuromuscular junction" (the point where the nerve endings, which run from the central nervous system to the muscle, deliver the signal to fire) is often out of shape.

I've discovered that for some people, it takes a month of doing the reverse crunch and other exercises for the lower abs before they can really start to feel them flex. However, if they stick with it, and give it time, they will enjoy the rewards!

Cross Crunch

Start/Finish

How It's Done

Lie on your back, knees bent, and position your left leg so it is across your right knee. Then, put your left hand, palm down, next to your left hip, and place your right hand gently on the right side of your head. Be sure to keep your neck relaxed.

Take a deep breath, then focus your mind on flexing your abs and envision pushing your lower back down into the floor and let that contraction begin to pull your shoulders upward and inward. At this point, think about aiming your right elbow toward your left knee while you *slowly breathe out and continue to flex* the abs as hard as you can. Once you've reached a point where your shoulders and upper back have lifted off the floor, flex your abs intensely for a full count of "one-thousand-one, one-thousand-two." Then, breathe in and slowly return to the starting position. Complete 12 to 15 repetitions in that position, then reverse sides so your right leg is across your left leg, your left hand is touching the left side of your head, and your right hand is palm down next to your right hip. Perform another set from that position.

Midpoint

Overview

This exercise works the muscles of Region 1 and Region 3 very effectively. And, it's an exercise that can be done at home or virtually anywhere, as it requires no equipment.

By placing one leg across another and putting the opposite hand behind the head, you create a slightly twisted torso, which brings the oblique muscles into action. Remember, to develop that narrow, sculpted midsection, you have to work the obliques, not just the front of the abs.

Once again, it is vitally important that this exercise be done slowly and with a great deal of mental focus.

Also remember that you do not need to bring the elbow all the way up to the knee—just aim the elbow toward the knee and contract the abs until you lift the upper back off the floor.

Training Tip

One variation I often use with the cross crunch is to place one hand across the belly and tap it (using touch training, which increases intensity) on the oblique muscles.

Decline Crunch

How It's Done

Position yourself on a decline bench, set at about a 30° angle. Sit so your upper body is perpendicular to the bench, not the floor. Place your hands at the sides of your head, and be sure not to tuck your chin all the way into your chest. It's best to relax your neck and keep the tension in the abs.

Slowly curl your chest toward your thighs while you focus on contracting the upper abs as hard as you can. Breathe out on the way up and flex for a count of two seconds when you reach a position where your elbows are about six to eight inches from your knees. Don't sit up so far that your elbows touch your knees because in that position there is no longer any resistance on your abs.

After you contract in the top position, slowly return to the starting point, take a deep breath, and repeat.

Start/Finish

Midpoint

Overview

The decline crunch is an excellent exercise for Region 1. It offers a unique and highly effective range of motion for flexing the upper abs.

It is very important to remember that while doing this exercise, you should *not* go all the way back and lay down on the decline bench and then curl all the way forward and do a sit-up. Unfortunately, a lot of people don't know that, and they end up experiencing a lower back injury, and they also end up putting too much stress on another group of muscles—those hip flexors—which help tie the upper body to the lower body.

Our objective on this exercise can be achieved with a very focused but small range of motion. From the time you sit down on the bench, you'll want to lean back just enough so you can feel your abs flexing, then, when you perform the exercise, come forward just enough that you can squeeze down on your abdominal muscles. Flexing and really concentrating on contracting the upper abs while you slowly go forward and back on the decline bench is a great way to build up these muscles. It's not complicated. Just follow the proper form, give it your best effort, and you'll enjoy good results!

Training Tip

A lot of people perform the decline crunch with their hands in front of their bodies, resting on their collar bones or chests. I've tried that variation, but I have found it doesn't provide as good a contraction as performing this exercise with the hands resting gently on the sides or behind the head.

Reverse Decline Crunch

How It's Done

To start with, lie back on a decline bench, and firmly hold onto the sides of the bench right behind your head, keeping your head still and your vision focused straight up. Then, raise your legs up off the floor and bring them to a point where they're just about perpendicular with the bench. Keep your feet together and your toes slightly pointed up. (You don't need to point the toes straight out.) Keep your legs straight, but do not lock your knees, which activates the hamstrings and takes some of the emphasis off the abs.

Now, take a deep breath and slowly begin curling your hips toward your shoulders. Don't just try to lift your legs straight up. The best way to activate the abdominal muscles is to *curl the hips toward the shoulders,* which brings the lower body upward and inward! Slowly breathe out while you continue to contract the lower abdominal muscles and keep going until your hips and lower back are off the bench. Then, hold this contracted position for a full count of two seconds.

After you've contracted your abs in the top position for two seconds, slowly lower yourself back to the starting point, relax for a moment, take a breath, and then do it again.

Start/Finish

Midpoint

Training Tip

It's slightly easier to perform this exercise with your knees bent rather than straight. If you're just getting started, try it this way, and as your lower abs become stronger and stronger, use the straight-leg position.

Overview

I first became aware of this exercise when I saw Sylvester Stallone doing it in one of his training scenes in the movie *Rocky III.* He was so lean and muscular, and his abs were so ripped, I could hardly wait to try it! And man oh man, when I learned how to do this exercise the right way, I felt like my belly had been used as a human punching bag! (It was a "good" type of soreness, if you know what I mean—the type of soreness that lets you know your workout worked!)

The reverse decline crunch is a very intense exercise that works Region 2, the lower abs. You will need an appropriate decline bench to perform this exercise. You can typically find this kind of bench at most commercial gyms.

As with virtually all of the ab exercises I do, the key for me is to go slowly and be determined to get something out of every single repetition. The way I see it, if all you're doing is going through the motions, why even bother doing it? Remember, it's *quality* not quantity that counts, especially when it comes to ab training!

While performing this exercise, it's important to remember to hold onto the bench tightly with your hands but not to flex the arms and shoulders and allow them to help curl your lower body upward. Also, it's important not to bring your legs up over your head into a full "jackknife" position, as that decreases rather than increases the effectiveness of this exercise.

Decline Twist

How It's Done

Using a decline bench, set at about a 30° angle, position yourself with your feet locked in. Your upper body should be perpendicular to the bench, so you have to contract your abs just to remain in place. Put your hands on each side of your head, just behind your ears. Don't lock your fingers.

From the starting position, slowly contract your left oblique (the muscle on the left side of your waist) while you twist your torso to the right, *moving your left elbow toward your right knee.* Breathe out and slowly and intensely contract the oblique. When you reach a position where your left elbow is almost touching your right knee, hold that position and flex for a count of "one-thousand-one, one-thousand-two." Then slowly untwist and return to the starting position but *keep the ab muscles flexed the whole time!*

The next rep, simply reverse the procedure, contracting your right oblique and bringing your right elbow toward your left knee. Continue alternating throughout the set.

Start/Finish

Midpoint

Overview

This is an *excellent* exercise I've used for years to define both Regions 1 and 3 of my abs. I use an alternating, twisting motion on a decline bench to contract the obliques and work the upper abs. This exercise is unique because it keeps the abs under constant tension and stress when done with the proper form.

The position of your head and neck are especially important in this exercise. Visualize holding a tennis ball between your chin and chest. This is where your head should remain. Do not tuck your chin into your chest, or you will put unnecessary strain on the neck.

I don't think I can emphasize enough that ab training should be done with strict form. I see abs trained incorrectly more than any other muscle group. Know what you are doing before you go to the gym, please. And *concentrate* during the exercise and give what you are doing your full, undivided attention!

Training Tip

On the decline bench, *never* allow your torso to go back beyond perpendicular to the bench. When you do (which many people think they are supposed to do), the stress shifts from the abdominal muscles to the hip flexors and lower back and may cause injury.

Bench Crunch

How It's Done

To begin this exercise, simply lie on the floor with your feet positioned atop a bench (or chair). Your knees should be bent at a 90° angle. Place your hands gently on the sides of your head and take a deep breath. Then, concentrate on flexing the upper abdominal muscles, pushing your lower back into the floor, and slowly curl your shoulders toward your knees as you breathe out. Aim your elbows toward your knees, flexing the ab muscles more with each inch your elbows move upward and inward.

When your shoulders and upper back have curled up off the floor and your elbows are six to eight inches from your knees, hold that position for a count of "one-thousand-one, one-thousand-two" and *flex those abs while pushing down with your lower back!* Then, slowly return to the starting position while you breathe in. Pause for a moment, and then repeat.

Start/Finish

Midpoint

Overview

This variation of the basic ab crunch is one I've made a part of my regular training routine for years. By simply positioning your feet on a bench, it puts more emphasis on the upper abs and takes pressure off the lower back. It also helps keep the hip flexors from being activated.

It's very important to just rest your feet on top of the bench and not put them under the bench, and use them for leverage to try to help you "sit up." That old-fashioned technique has caused a lot of unnecessary strain in people's lower backs. Please note that the crunch is not the same as that old-fashioned sit-up you might have done in Junior High PE class. The crunch is a much more focused, safer, and effective way to exercise the abdominal muscles. Please, *if you're doing sit-ups now, stop,* and don't let anyone ever tell you they're an effective ab exercise—they're outdated and not the right way to train.

The bench crunch, on the other hand, is one of the best exercises for stimulating the abdominal muscles and developing that six pack.

Training Tip

For variation, I'll often take one hand off the side of my head, place it on the oblique muscle on the opposite side of my body, and perform a twisting ab crunch. For example, *aiming my right elbow toward my left knee.* This helps develop the muscles in Region 3 as well as Region 1.

Cable Crunch

Overview

Like the basic ab crunch, this exercise works Region 1, the upper abs. The ability to adjust resistance and intensity with the amount of weight makes this ab exercise one of my favorites.

Cable crunches feel different than floor crunches because the resistance from the cable is constant. With floor crunches, the resistance (due to the angle of the body and the pull of gravity) reduces as your body rises.

Please do not use too much weight on this exercise. Select a weight that allows your abs to flex for 12 to 15 reps. Using too much weight may work something called the "psoas" muscles, also called the "hip flexors." It can also hurt the lower back.

The cable crunch, performed properly, can really build and define your abs and help create that six pack!

How It's Done

Using a high cable pulley, attach a rope handle. I prefer the rope because it allows for the most natural grip and freedom of motion. If a rope is not available, a small V-grip handle can be used as well. Select a light weight at first.

The cable crunch is just like the ab crunch, flipped over. Instead of lying on your back, you are on your knees, facing down, where you begin in a kneeling position. Your upper legs should be at a 90° angle to the floor, and your back slightly arched. Hold the ends of the rope with each hand positioned above your head.

Keeping your pelvis and lower back stationary, begin to pull the rope downward and inward toward your knees as you breathe out. Stop before you reach the floor or your knees and *contract the abs with all the intensity you can and hold it* for a full two seconds. Then, slowly allow the weight to "uncurl" your body, pulling you back to the starting point, slightly arching the back and stretching the abs. Repeat with focused intensity, taking it slow and giving each rep all you've got to give!

Start/Finish

Midpoint

Training Tip

A variation of the cable crunch to work Regions 1 *and* 3 is to grip the rope in one hand and perform a twisting crunch. Be sure to use less weight when you try this exercise.

Swiss Ball Crunch

How It's Done

To start with, sit down on the Swiss ball, just like you'd sit on a chair. Your feet should be shoulder width apart. Take a step forward with your right foot, then your left, while you slowly lean back. The ball will roll forward just enough that you will be positioned comfortably with your shoulders and hips touching the ball. Put your hands gently behind your head.

Now, focus on contracting the abs while you begin curling the shoulders up toward the hips. Be sure to move slowly, taking two seconds on the way up, while you breathe out. Hold the contracted position for a full count of two, and then return to the starting position. Take a deep breath, then repeat.

You really should not stretch back at more than a 30° angle nor come up to more than a 30° angle, which is the range the abdominal muscles are actually flexing.

Start/Finish

Midpoint

Training Tip

Don't sit too far forward on the Swiss ball, which will drop your hips and reduce the effectiveness of the exercise!

Overview

Of all the ab-training exercise devices and equipment that have come out over the last few years, the simple "Swiss ball" (it's like a big, heavy-duty beach ball) is my favorite! It allows you to exercise in very natural positions and makes it possible to stretch the back and abs more than you would be able to if you were lying on a flat bench or on the floor. This gives you a greater range of motion and works the abdominal muscles more than the basic floor crunch.

Also, because the ball wants to roll in one direction or another while you're doing the exercises, it forces you to use "stabilizer muscles" (think of them as small muscles between big muscles), which contribute to functional strength, which is the type of muscle strength you need for recreational sports and other activities besides lifting weights.

Exercising on a Swiss ball helps development of all the muscles of the midsection, even though this exercise works primarily Region 1.

The Swiss ball is a *great* piece of home exercise equipment. Give it a try if you haven't already!

Swiss Ball Leg Lift

How It's Done

The first thing you need to do for this exercise is position a Swiss ball in front of something sturdy you can hold onto, like a power rack, a Smith machine, or a very heavy-duty exercise bench. Position the Swiss ball a couple of feet in front of whatever you're going to hold onto, then sit down on the Swiss ball, take a step forward with your right foot, a step forward with your left foot, and lie back. Then, extend your arms behind your head and grasp whatever you're going to use to anchor your body. Make sure your hips and shoulders are positioned on the Swiss ball, and that you're not too far back or too far forward. Bend your knees a bit and slightly point your toes.

Now, take a deep breath, and begin contracting your lower abs, lifting your legs, and curling your hips up toward your shoulders. Be sure to keep your neck in a relaxed position with your vision focused upward toward the ceiling. Continue to slowly raise your legs until your toes are pointed straight up, with your legs at a 90° angle. Then, *very* slowly, lower your legs to the starting position. The slower you lower your legs on this exercise, the better.

Once you've reached the starting position, take a deep breath, get your balance, and lift those legs again.

Start/Finish

Midpoint

Overview

This is an absolutely outstanding exercise for Region 2, the lower abs! Like most Swiss ball exercises, it allows you to work through a greater range of motion, activate more muscle fibers, and is *very intense* when performed properly.

The Swiss ball will have a tendency to roll just slightly to the left and right, forward and back. Every time it does, you'll feel a different area of the muscles in your midsection contracting to help you catch your balance. This is a good thing! However, if you simply swing your legs up and down, you may lose your balance and fall off! So please, go slow, especially when you're lowering your legs. And, hold on tight with your hands to something sturdy.

I do not recommend you do this exercise with additional weight. (I've seen some people at the gym doing it with a dumbbell between their feet.) This just isn't necessary. If you learn to contract the abdominal muscles intensely, you'll get all the work you need without putting a weight between your feet, which, in actuality, only makes the hip flexors and lower back more involved in this exercise.

Training Tip

The morning after you do this exercise, your lower abs may be so sore that you are compelled to send me a nasty note, rich with colorful expletives. If so, I can be reached at www.BestABS.com. ☺

Swiss Ball Side Crunch

How It's Done

First, sit down on a Swiss ball and get your balance. Then, take a step forward with your right foot, take a step forward with your left foot, and slowly lean back on the ball. Then, with your feet shoulder width apart, rotate your hips to the left so that your feet are facing that direction, but your torso is twisted and your shoulders are still facing upward. Now, place your right hand gently at the right side of your head, and place your left hand on your right oblique.

Pause for a moment, get your balance, take a deep breath, then slowly begin to contract the muscles on the right side of your midsection while you begin to breathe out and move your right elbow upward and forward. Continue to curl your upper body toward

Start/Finish

Midpoint

your right hip, moving in a direction where your right arm is in line with your right leg.

Once you have lifted the right shoulder blade area of your upper back completely off of the Swiss ball, pause and flex the muscles on the right side of your midsection as hard as you possibly can while you count to yourself, "One-thousand-one, one-thousand-two." Then, slowly begin to lower yourself back to the starting position while you breathe in. It's important to still flex the muscle on the way back until you return to the starting position, where you should relax and pause for a moment, before you repeat the exercise for 12 to 15 repetitions.

After you've completed a set with your feet facing to the left, take the opposite position, your feet facing to the right, put your left hand at the left side of your head and your right hand on your left oblique and perform 12 to 15 reps for the other side.

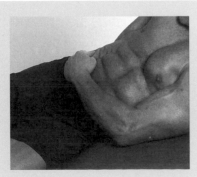

Training Tip

While slowly curling your upper body into the side crunch position, try tapping the oblique muscle with the hand resting on it. This technique, called "touch training," helps increase the muscle contraction by helping you focus more intensely on the muscle we're trying to develop. You can utilize touch training in many exercises where you have one hand free.

Wow! That's what I said after the first time I performed this Swiss ball exercise. It really hits Region 3, the oblique muscles, in a way that the standard floor crunch can't. One of the reasons this exercise is so effective is that the arc of the Swiss ball allows you to begin the exercise in a pre-stretched position, which *doubles the range of motion* and therefore significantly enhances the time the obliques are under tension.

Another benefit to doing this exercise on a Swiss ball is that because it wants to roll a bit from side to side, I found I was flexing not just the oblique muscles but the lower abs, the upper abs, and the entire midsection! When you first start exercising with the Swiss ball, you may feel a bit clumsy and awkward, but don't worry about it—I'm still a bit clumsy and awkward on the Swiss ball too. One of the things I've learned over the years is that the more coordination an exercise requires, the more muscles it works, and the more effective it is!

A few years ago, virtually no one knew what a Swiss ball was except for a few very well informed strength and conditioning coaches. Now, you'll find this great piece of exercise equipment in many gyms and virtually all athletic training rooms. The side crunch is just one of many exercises I perform on my Swiss ball, which is a part of my home gym.

Hanging Leg Lift

Start/Finish

Midpoint

Overview

Properly performed, this exercise targets Region 2, the lower abs. And while I have to admit this exercise can be effective, it has always been a bit challenging for me. You see, over the years I've had several shoulder injuries. None of them serious enough that I would need surgery, but they have been serious enough that I have to be extremely careful how I position my shoulders during exercises so as to not aggravate the inner workings of that complicated and vitally important upper body area specifically known as the "rotator cuff." For that reason, I only do the hanging leg raise once in a while. But that doesn't mean it won't be an effective exercise for you unless you, too, have had a shoulder injury.

You can perform this exercise with your knees slightly bent or almost straight—slightly bent is easier and is good if you're just beginning to strengthen the lower abs.

A common mistake I see people make while performing this exercise at the gym is, once again, they simply do it too fast and end up doing little more than swinging their legs up and down, forward and back, and doing very little to stimulate the abdominal muscles. This exercise must be done s-l-o-w-l-y for it to be effective!

How It's Done

To begin, hang from a pull-up bar with a shoulder-width grip, or utilize arm straps that allow you to hold your body weight with your upper arms, instead of just the grip of your hands. Next, allow your legs to hang down, keeping them very relaxed so your knees are bent a bit and your toes are slightly pointed.

From here, take a deep breath, and begin to lift your legs upward, while you focus on contracting your abs. Breathe out slowly, continue lifting your legs, while you roll your hips upward. Continue to lift until your feet are pointed straight out and hold that contracted position for a full count of "one-thousand-one, one-thousand-two." Then, slowly lower your legs to the starting position, take a deep breath, and repeat.

Training Tip

Keeping your toes slightly pointed while you're lifting your legs can reduce the amount of work being done by the hip flexors and increase the lower ab work.

Ab Vacuum

How It's Done

To begin, lie on your back with your knees bent, feet flat on the floor, and your hands at the sides of your hips, palms facing down. Rest your head on the floor and keep your vision focused upward or even close your eyes gently. Now, breathe out, *exhaling every last bit of air* you can from your lungs, and hold it! Don't breathe in through your nose or your mouth for a moment. Instead, pull your belly in and up, as far as you can and hold it for a count of, "one-thousand-one, one-thousand-two." Then, relax, and breathe in again. Lie there, take a couple breaths, and then repeat.

This exercise is a bit like a disappearing act for the midsection. It is a totally different feeling from flexing your abs. You're truly using inner muscles in a way that no other midsection exercise does. The ab vacuum is an exercise you perform by concentrating your mind. You can't "muscle" your way through it.

Start/Finish

Midpoint

Overview

The ab vacuum is very effective but almost a completely unknown ab exercise. Because it helps strengthen a muscle called the *transverse abdominis* (I call it the "inner abs"), it in turn helps improve the strength, as well as the look, of all three of your "outer ab" regions.

Performed regularly, the ab vacuum can help you reduce the size of your waistline as much or more than any other ab exercise! This is an exercise that can really help you flatten the belly and give you that strong, athletic look with a narrow waist and good posture. When these inner ab muscles are weak, the belly distends—it just kind of hangs out. Of course, all of the exercises we do for the abdominal muscles will help resolve that problem, but this one, for me, has been my all-time favorite!

You can do it anywhere, and you need no equipment. However, it will take practice—possibly weeks of practice (doing it three times a week)—in order to begin to create a vacuum and pull the muscles in, almost tucking them up under the rib cage. When you perform this exercise regularly and you strengthen the inner abs, you'll be able to perform all your other ab exercises with more focused intensity. You'll feel the difference in a matter of weeks.

If you put the time and effort into practicing and then mastering this exercise, it may seem as if you reversed gravity and what was starting to look like a landslide in your midsection is put back in place, appearing more youthful, athletic, healthy, and heroic!

Training Tip

After you've developed the ability to do the vacuum lying on the floor (which may take several weeks of practice), try doing it standing up, with your hands behind your head and your elbows pointed upward. This is even more intense as you're working against gravity.

The exercises I described in this chapter are my absolute favorites for developing all of the major regions of the midsection. If you'd like to see even more exercise demonstrations, be sure to visit me online at www.BestABS.com.

Now, we don't do all of these ab exercises in every workout. What I do is select one exercise for each of the three regions and combine them in what I call a "triple series" manner, where I perform one exercise, then go straight to another, and another. For example, I might train Region 1 with the basic crunch for 15 repetitions, and then go directly to hip-ups for Region 2 and perform 15 repetitions, and then go directly to the side crunch for Region 3 and do 15 repetitions. Then I'd rest for a minute and repeat that series of exercises for a total of three sets. That's how simple putting together an effective ab-training workout can be. As you've now learned, it's a combination of choosing the *right exercises* and performing them with *proper form and intensity* that makes a difference!

I perform a series of exercises like this no more than three times a week. I usually train abs after my cardio workouts. Occasionally I'll do an ab workout like the one I described above in the evening, while I'm listening to music or watching the nightly news. There are a number of different variations and styles of training I use for ab workouts that I'll continue to teach you in the chapters that follow.

However, I want to point out once again that performing these ab exercises alone will not give you a lean, muscular midsection. You have to lower your bodyfat with proper nutrition and by exercising all the major muscle groups of the body and doing cardio exercise as well.

Now, if my ABSolution Program was "typical" and similar to what is out there in the market, this book would be over right now. However, we still have work to do! Remember what I shared with you at the beginning of this book—I am going to cover *everything* you need to know to build your own absolutely amazing abs.

CHAPTER NINE

The Best of the Rest

To build your abs, *build your body*. To build your body, you have to do a lot more than crunches and leg lifts. In fact, you have to apply the same type of focused intensity and determination to strengthening every major muscle group in your body to really get in great shape. Make no mistake, I would not look anything like I do in these photos if I were doing just direct abdominal work! And if I were to lead you to believe anything other than that, I'd be as guilty as all of those so-called businessmen and "experts" out there promoting the latest quick-fix scam for sculpting washboard abs.

I cannot and will not mislead you. That's not what this book is about. My intention is to provide you with all the information you need to build a truly great-looking, healthy, and strong physique, complete with defined abs.

In an effort to follow through on my promise, in this chapter I'll share with you specific instructions for how to perform my favorite weight-training exercises for the other major muscle regions: chest, shoulders, back, biceps, triceps, and legs.

For these weight-training exercises to be effective, you need to apply the fundamental principle of progressive resistance training to your workouts, as we previously discussed in this book. Also, remember that it is during our workouts that we prime the muscle (not pulverize it!), and that during the rest and recovery period (when you're not working out) is when the body performs its "magic" and rebuilds stronger, better, and healthier than it was before.

I train with weights just three times a week for about an hour or less each workout. When I perform the right exercises at the proper intensity, that's all I need, and despite what many people think, that's all you'll need too.

Please review the information I'm going to share with you in this chapter carefully. You'll notice that most of the exercises I do are basic, just like my favorite ab exercises, but if you follow the proper form and train *intensely and intelligently*, you too will experience excellent results!

Start/Finish

Midpoint

Dumbbell Bench Press

This exercise works primarily the chest, but also the shoulders and triceps. To perform this exercise, you need only a flat bench and a set of dumbbells. To begin, pick up the dumbbells, keeping your feet flat on the floor, and lie back on the bench. One of the keys to doing the proper form on this exercise is to keep the weight over the collar bones. Don't lift it up over your face or your belly—keep it over your chest. Press the weight up while you breathe out, hold it for a count of one, then lower it slowly. Pause, then press it back up. That's how simple it is!

Incline Dumbbell Flyes

This is an *excellent* exercise to work the upper chest muscles and also the front of the shoulders. What you need is an incline bench and two dumbbells. Lie back, feet flat on the floor. Lift the weight up slowly in an arc, as if you were putting your arms around someone. The palms should be facing each other all the way up. Pause at the top, then slowly lower the weight in an arc with the elbows slightly bent. Stretch to the point where your hands are in line with your shoulders. Don't stretch too far on this one, or you may put too much stress on the shoulder muscles and joints.

Start/Finish   **Midpoint**

Start/Finish

Midpoint

Barbell Bench Press

This exercise works the muscles of the chest, shoulders, and triceps. To begin, lie on a bench and firmly position your feet flat on the floor a little more than shoulder width apart. Arch your back slightly, but keep your hips on the bench. Using a grip wider than your shoulders, hold the barbell, with your elbows locked, over the middle of your chest. Then, slowly lower the weight to the middle of your chest. Pause for a count of one when the bar just barely makes contact with your upper chest. Then, *without bouncing* the weight off your chest, push the barbell up over the middle of your chest until your arms are straight and your elbows are locked out. Breathe in on the way down and out on the way up.

Standing Triceps Extension

This exercise works the back of your arms and your shoulders. To begin, put your feet about shoulder-width apart, take one dumbbell and raise it above your head. Rest both palms against the dumbbell with the elbows high and together. Then, slowly lower the dumbbell down behind your head, hold it for a moment in the fully stretched position before pressing it back up. It's important on this exercise to breathe in on the way down, breathe out on the way up. The dumbbell triceps extension is one of those exercises that's a little bit awkward at first, but it's one of the most effective exercises you can do!

Start/Finish   **Midpoint**

Start/Finish

Midpoint

Reverse-Grip Cable Extension

This exercise works the back of the arms and the lower abs. Using a high cable or lat pulldown machine, place both hands on the bar, gripping it slightly wider than shoulder width apart with your palms up. Now, rotate the bar downward, straightening your arms. *Fully contract the triceps and flex*, holding that position for a count of "one thousand one." Then let the bar come back to the top position, pause for a moment, and repeat.

Start/Finish

Lying Dumbbell Extension

This exercise works the triceps. To begin, lie down on a flat bench with a dumbbell in each hand, positioned over your forehead. Next, lower the dumbbells to the sides of your head. It's important you *go slow* on this exercise and pause for a count of one in both the fully stretched and contracted positions. Breathe in on the way down; breathe out on the way up. Done correctly, this is one of the best triceps exercises you can do!

Midpoint

Start/Finish

Midpoint

Standing Dumbbell Press

This exercise develops primarily the shoulder muscles and also works the triceps and upper back. To begin, hold two dumbbells, right at the base of the shoulders. Then press the weights straight up, overhead. Breathe out on the way up; breathe in on the way down. Once again, we're pressing it up slowly, letting it down slowly. Make sure you lift the weights right over the head, in line with the shoulders! Don't let the weights move out in front of your body or back. It's very important not to lean back on this exercise, keep the tension on the shoulders and not on the lower back.

Dumbbell Side Raise

This exercise is for the shoulders. Start with the dumbbells right down by your sides. Then raise them up to a point where they're even with the shoulders. Your palms should be facing down, so it works the shoulders, not the biceps. Keep your arms almost perfectly straight—bring them right out to your sides—forming almost an iron cross. Do not lean forward or back! Keep the whole body still; just lift with your delts. Pause for a moment at the top, and let the weight down slowly.

Start/Finish

Midpoint

Start/Finish

Midpoint

Bent-Over Side Raise

This exercise works the upper back and shoulders. What you do is hold a pair of dumbbells with your feet a little less than shoulder-width apart. Lean over at the hips until your upper body is parallel with the floor. At that point, raise the dumbbells straight out to your sides until your hands are about the same height as your shoulders. Hold them up in that top position for just a moment. It's very important you *don't raise your upper body* while you're doing this exercise. And you also don't want to hunch your back. Keep your back flat. Breathe in as you raise the weight and out as you lower it. The slower you go on this exercise, the better!

One-Arm Dumbbell Row

This exercise works primarily the muscles in the back, but also the biceps. To begin, put one knee on a flat bench and support your upper body with the hand you're not going to lift the weight with. In the other hand, pick up a dumbbell and begin to lift it while you breathe out. Keep the dumbbell parallel to the floor while you pull it up as far as you can—to the point where it about touches the rib cage. Hold it for a count of one and then *lower it slowly*. To keep this exercise safe and effective, you need to keep the focus on "rowing" the weight, without moving the upper body.

Start/Finish

Midpoint

Dumbbell Pullover

Start/Finish

Midpoint

This exercise helps develop your back muscles, as well as your chest, triceps, and abs. This is one of the *best* but most overlooked exercises for building your upper body! To begin, lie across a flat bench with only your upper back on the bench. Your feet should be about shoulder width apart and flat on the floor. Now, reach back and flatten your hands against the inside upper plate of one end of a dumbbell, which should be positioned "on end" on the floor next to the bench. Keeping your hips low, slowly lift the dumbbell while you breathe out. Hold it above your forehead for a count of one, then lower the weight, in an arc, while you breathe in very deeply. Then repeat.

Reverse-Grip High Pulldown

Start/Finish   **Midpoint**

This exercise works primarily the muscles of the back and also the biceps. Begin by positioning yourself at a cable pulldown machine. Adjust the seat so your knees rest firmly against the pads above them. Reach up with your palms facing you, and grab the bar just outside shoulder width. From this stretched position, pull the bar down slowly to your upper chest while you contract your back muscles and breathe out. Keep your elbows in close to your body. Your back should be arched slightly, your chest high, chin up, and your abs and lower back tight. After you hold the bar in the contracted position for a moment, let the weight up, resisting it as you straighten your arms. Take a deep breath and repeat.

Start/Finish   Midpoint

Incline Dumbbell Curl

This exercise works the biceps. To begin, sit down on an incline bench with a dumbbell in each hand, with the palms facing forward. Keep your chin up, and your upper body firmly positioned against the bench. Curl the weights up toward your chest, nice and slow. Contract the biceps muscles as hard as you can at the top and hold it for a count of one. Then lower the weights for a count of two. One of the best ways to increase the effectiveness of this exercise is to *let that weight down very slowly!*

Barbell Curl

This exercise works the biceps. Start with your hands shoulder-width apart, underhand grip, on a barbell. Stand up straight with shoulders squared and with your feet shoulder-width apart. Without leaning back or swinging the weight, curl the bar up toward your chest in an arc while you breathe out. Keep your elbows stationary and close to your sides. Bring the weight up as high as you can, and focus on holding the contraction at the top. *Lower the weight slowly* along the same path, resisting all the way down until your arms are nearly straight but you can still feel a contraction in the biceps. Hold that position for a moment, take a deep breath, and then begin your next rep.

Start/Finish   Midpoint

Start/Finish

Midpoint

Leg Press

This exercise works *all* the major muscles of the lower body! To begin, position yourself on a leg press machine with your feet about shoulder width apart. Then, slowly lower the weight to the point where your thighs almost make contact with your upper body. Hold it there for a moment, then press the weight back up while you breathe out. Don't "lock out" at the top—keep your legs just slightly bent.

Barbell Squat

This exercise works all the major muscle groups of the lower body: the quadriceps, the hamstrings, the hips, and the calves. It's an extremely demanding exercise! What you do is position your feet slightly wider than shoulder-width apart. Rest the barbell on the back of the shoulders, not on your neck, and hold it in position with your hands. Keeping your chin up, eyes looking forward, and back straight, simply bend your knees and lower your hips until your thighs are parallel with the floor, pause, and lift the weight back up. Breathe in on the way down, breathe out on the way up. To get the best leg workout on this exercise, keep your back as straight as you can—do not lean over.

Start/Finish   **Midpoint**

I've done literally thousands of hours of weight training during my life, and I intend to do thousands of hours more. "Pound for pound" it's the best type of exercise you can do! It not only burns calories and helps stimulate muscle growth but it also strengthens bones, tendons, and ligaments; even the heart and the rest of the cardiovascular system benefit from proper weight training. However, it's important to know when to say when... it's important to know the right amount of weight training needed to prime the muscles and stimulate a positive adaptation. A lot of people get eager and overdo it when it comes to weight training. What I've discovered over the last two decades is something scientific research has confirmed in recent years: *less is more*. What I mean is that using the proper exercises, with the correct form, with a high level of focused intensity produces better results than long, agonizing, two-hour weight-training workouts. Weight training is not an endurance activity. The best workouts are short and sweet. Remember, *it's quality, not quantity!*

Here's an example of how I structure a workout: I'll do five sets of the dumbbell bench press and three sets of dumbbell flyes on an incline bench. I start with a set of 15 repetitions for my first set, then I increase the weight, perform 12 repetitions, then 10, then 8, then 6, increasing the weight between each set. I rest about a minute between each set. For dumbbell flyes, I do 3 sets of 10 repetitions, then train shoulders and triceps, performing 3 to 4 sets of 2 different exercises per muscle group, varying between 6 and 12 repetitions per set.

"Weight training is not an endurance activity. The best workouts are short and sweet."

During my next weight-training workout, I'll train my back, biceps, and legs, doing just two exercises for each muscle group. Leg exercises require so much energy and burn so many calories and are so grueling, I found that by doing two exercises twice a week, I'm getting good results, and I'm also feeling more energetic and stronger. I've tried training legs three times a week, but it was so exhausting, it led to overtraining. Remember, there's a fine line between priming and pulverizing your muscles. And, over the years, I've had to learn to keep my ambition in check and realize I'm far from super human; like everyone else, I can recover from only a certain amount of intense exercise.

Later in the book, I'll give you more examples of how I structure my weight-training workouts. And for more exercise demonstrations, visit me at www.BestABS.com.

Remember that all the exercises I've taught you about in this chapter burn fat, strengthen the entire skeletal muscle system, and help you build muscular, defined abs. That's often not what people who are looking for the "easy way" to rock-hard abs want to hear, but it's the truth—it takes hard work to build a great body!

CHAPTER TEN

Let's
HIIT It

I learned just about all I needed to know about effective cardio exercise during my first year of Little League football. I was nine years old, playing for a team called the Golden Eagles. On offense, I was a running back, and on defense, I played linebacker. Not that it really mattered much what position anyone on the team played on game day—as soon as each play started, we'd all just run around and chase the one with the football. My friends and I had a blast!

I can't recall exactly how many games we won or lost that season; however, one thing I will never forget is what I learned about intense cardio exercise that year. At the end of every practice, our coach would line us up on the goal line, have us sprint as fast as we could for 40 yards, allow us a very short rest, then he'd line us up and make us sprint back to the goal line, giving it *everything* we had. Those "wind sprints" were brutal! They were absolutely, positively so intense that by the time we were done with about ten sprints, we would all be so tired we'd have to kneel down and gasp for air before we could stand up and walk off the field. That was my introduction to cardio exercise.

As an adult, when I began studying exercise science, what I discovered is that our coach was having us do "High-Intensity Interval Training" or "HIIT." That's a type of exercise where you do a short, high-intensity burst of activity, followed by a brief period of rest, followed by another burst, and so on. In research, scientists have discovered that HIIT is remarkably effective—it significantly improves endurance and overall fitness.

I don't think coach followed the scientific literature all that closely; in fact, come to think of it, the only "six pack" he focused on was the one he kept in a cooler in the trunk of his car. I do give him credit for knowing what worked, even if he didn't apply it himself. I suspect, through his years of experience as a former ballplayer and then as a coach, he learned that intense interval exercise helped increase athletic performance.

I first wrote about high-intensity interval training several years ago in *Muscle Media* magazine. Since then, I've received letters from literally hundreds of people who have traded in their hour of low-intensity, long-duration, boring, marginally effective cardio for an intense 10 to 20 minutes of interval training and have not only saved time but significantly improved their results.

One of the primary reasons high-intensity interval training works is because it doesn't just speed up your metabolism (the rate your body burns calories) during exercise, but it keeps the metabolic rate increased for hours afterwards. Low-intensity cardio does not offer this benefit. This has been shown in numerous scientific studies. Also, since it doesn't require as much time, it's more practical. I've noticed that people tend to stick with it more consistently—it's easier to fit 20 minutes of cardio exercise into your schedule than it is an hour, which means you're much more likely to make it a regular habit. You can't overlook that. You have to make these workouts a part of your lifestyle: you have to do them consistently for them to work!

One of the most powerful benefits of this type of training that you won't find reported in any of the scientific literature but one I can certainly guarantee you'll experience is *it will force you to develop your inner strength*—your tolerance for intense exercise. And that's something that complements your weight-training workouts. When you're performing

"One of the most powerful benefits of this type of training is that *it will force you to develop your inner strength*—your tolerance for intense exercise."

interval training with true intensity, your ability to tolerate physical pain is expanded. This is a good thing! Rather than doing the opposite—jogging at a low-intensity level, sitting on a stationary bike for an hour without ever pushing yourself... that teaches you to exercise within a certain comfort zone, and that is a *bad habit*.

One of the things I used to notice about people I was helping with their workouts is that when I asked them to turn up the intensity or lift more weight on a certain exercise, they'd quickly reply, "Shawn, I can't..." That was what they perceived. They really thought they could lift only a certain amount of weight or perform at a certain intensity on their cardio because that is what they had been training themselves to believe.

When I started teaching people about HIIT back in 1996, some thought it couldn't possibly work. But, over the years, that controversy has subsided, and now people are more interested in *how* I "HIIT it" rather than why. So, with that in mind, let me give you some examples of how simple (I didn't say it was easy... I said it was simple) a HIIT workout can be.

One of the ways I perform high-intensity interval training, especially in the spring and summer, is that I walk down to a park near my house, and I do wind sprints, like we used to back in the old days, during football practice. What I do is start with jogging for a couple minutes to get my body warmed up, then I mark off a distance of about 40 or 50 yards, and I simply sprint across the field. Then I rest for less than a minute and turn around and sprint back. I rest again before doing another sprint, and so on. I'll do 10 to 15 these wind sprints, and that's it. I'm cooked. This is an *extremely intense* form of exercise, and if you have any doubts about that, I encourage you to give it a try before making the mistake of assuming it won't work for you like it has worked for me!

Another way I incorporate HIIT into my workouts is I'll run stairs. My favorite place to do that is an outdoor arena called Red Rocks Amphitheater, which is a couple miles from my home, just south of Golden, in the Colorado foothills. At Red Rocks, they have a huge flight of stairs. I don't run the whole thing: I have a section of about 40 steps where I do

my workout. What I do is walk up and down the stairs to get warmed up. Then I run up the stairs and walk back down. Then I run up the stairs again and walk back down. I do this 10 or 15 times. Not real high tech, is it? But, it is *brutally intense!*

While I'm running the stairs, not only am I getting a cardio workout, but the muscles in my legs are getting a workout—my hamstrings, calves, everything is burning. And, because my torso is constantly twisting and my arms are pumping, I'm getting a great ab workout too, especially in Region 3, the obliques. This is why I encourage people to get off the stationary bikes and StairMasters and do other types of cardio exercise more often. I think this is one of the things that has helped me stay in such good condition year after year—my workouts are intense, and I incorporate a lot of sprinting and stair climbing into my Program. This is a habit for me.

Here's another example: near my home, there's a trail called Falcon Ridge. During the warm weather, quite a few people from my neighborhood walk this path and hike the hill while I use it for HIIT workouts. Sometimes they're not sure what the heck I'm doing when I run past them on the way up, only to be walking back down the trail a minute later, and then run past them on the way back up. I just smile and say, "Hey, it's me again..." every time I pass them. They get a kick out of it, and *I get a killer workout!*

When I'm in Southern California visiting friends, I virtually never do cardio inside a gym. I'll go to the beach and do wind sprints. It is so much more effective than sitting inside on a stationary bike, peddling away, especially for building and toning your midsection.

Another form of HIIT that has worked well for me when I'm traveling is simply jumping rope. I bring a jump rope with me whenever I travel. It's very basic—I'll start by doing a couple minutes of rope jumping at a relatively slow pace to get my muscles warmed up. Then, I'll rest about 30 seconds, then skip rope at a relatively fast pace for a minute, rest 30 seconds, and so on.

The stationary bike is a "last-resort" HIIT workout that I perform when I can't get outside. The tension on the bike in my home gym is adjustable, so what I do is start with a couple minutes at a relatively low intensity level, then I crank up the intensity, push it *really hard* for a minute, then I lower the intensity to catch my breath, then I turn the intensity back up, then I lower it again to catch my breath. When I'm on the stationary bike, I picture myself sprinting, then resting, then sprinting, then resting. You get the idea. You can do the same thing on a treadmill, a StairMaster, or virtually any type of cardio equipment where you can adjust the intensity level manually.

Sometimes I'll use a stopwatch to keep track of my rest periods, but more often than not, I find myself resting just long enough to catch my breath, and then I sprint, jump rope, stair climb, hill run, etc. until I am out of breath—until I've really pushed myself! Then I'll walk, jog, or simply pace back and forth until I catch my breath again.

An effective HIIT workout can be as little as 10 minutes and rarely more than 20. If you're just beginning to train like this, you may burn out quickly—in as little as a few minutes. But if you stick with it, you'll notice you gain endurance and strength quickly.

I very often do my direct abdominal exercises after my HIIT workout. This is a great combination for me because I can do both an effective

> "HIIT training works on a physical level, and it also helps on a mental and even emotional level by helping you build *inner strength*."

cardio workout followed by my intense ab training, and it takes only about 30 to 40 minutes. I usually do this three times a week.

HIIT training works on a physical level to help you develop your muscles, improve your endurance, and burn fat, and it also helps on a mental and even emotional level by helping you build *inner strength*. Plus, it helps you save time, it's challenging enough to keep your interest, and you can do it just about anywhere. It really is an absolutely fantastic form of exercise, and when performed regularly, it will help you become leaner, healthier, and stronger in every way! What more could you want from cardio exercise?

CHAPTER ELEVEN

Putting It
All Together

Now we've reached the point where we're ready to put it all together. I've shared with you the mindset I approach ab training and overall fitness with. I've taught you how I nourish my success by eating the right balance of foods and supplements. I've also covered ab training, weightlifting, and high-intensity cardio. All of the essential elements are there. What we need now is a formula, a recipe, to put them all together. And that's what I'm going to give you in this chapter. By way of specific example, I'll guide you through my Program, showing you precisely when I exercise and how, when I eat, what I eat, and even what supplements I take.

As you review this information, keep in mind that the ABSolution Program is not an arbitrary system based on guesswork. It's based on sound, scientific principles, and it can benefit virtually every healthy adult, regardless of fitness level. I'm not saying the ABSolution Program is the only way to build a lean, muscular midsection, but when you follow my Program, you *will* get results.

The closer and more consistently you follow the principles of the ABSolution Program, the faster you will make progress. The more you adjust, alter, and "dink" with it, the more you're engaging in trial and error. That's like setting off on a journey with the intent of traveling from Point A to Point B (knowing where you started and where you want to go) and having a road map in your hand but not following it. Sure, you may get there, but you may not. The only way to be sure is to follow the map, carefully, closely, and consistently.

Now, before we go any further, I want to point out the importance of planning and preparation to success with this Program. There's an old saying, "If you fail to plan, you're planning to fail," and it is something that certainly applies to building your best abs, as well as many other areas in life. In fact, what I've discovered is planning and being prepared is an *essential* good habit. The opposite (not planning and not being prepared) is obviously a bad habit. In fact, that is the one habit that is causing many people to end up with 25 extra pounds of unwanted bodyfat to begin with.

Remember, your level of fitness isn't necessarily determined by your willpower, intelligence, nor merely genetics... it's habits that make us, and habits that break us.

So how do you incorporate the good habit of proper planning and preparation into the ABSolution Program? One of the most important "exercises" you can do is setting aside ten minutes each night, before you go to sleep, and writing in a journal. (It can be a day planner, a simple spiral notebook, a computer program—anything that you can journal entries in will do.) During this ten-minute "exercise session," what I recommend is that you write down your "ABSolution Intent" for the following day. State when you're going to work out, what foods and supplements you're going to consume, and when. It's not any more complicated than that. In fact, once you get in the habit of this, it won't even take you ten minutes. The importance of planning and preparation and journaling cannot be underestimated. Scientific studies show that people who keep an accurate, honest journal of their nutrition and exercise program are far more likely to succeed than people who don't.

So now, let's take a specific look at how I apply the principals of the ABSolution Program. In the pages that follow, you'll see my journal records and notes. You'll see my ab-training workouts, my cardio and weightlifting. You'll also see when I eat, what I eat, and what supplements I take. As you follow along with my specific examples, notice how I put it all together—how I carefully combine all the essential elements into one complete Program.

"The closer and more consistently you follow the principles of the ABSolution Program, the faster you will make progress."

ABSolution Worksheet

Name: Shawn Phillips   Date: May 6

Time	Planned Activity		Status ✔ = Done
6:00 a.m.		16 ounces of water	✔
	Supplement	Lean System 7 (3 capsules)	✔
		Cup of coffee	✔
6:20 a.m.	**Cardio Exercise**	HIIT workout—20 minutes on StairMaster	✔
6:45 a.m.	**AB Training**	Swiss Ball Crunch—3 x 15	✔
	Triple Series	Swiss Ball Leg Lift—3 x 15	✔
		Swiss Ball Side Crunch—3 x 15	✔
7:40 a.m.	**Breakfast**	8 egg white omelet with a little low-fat cheddar cheese	✔
		1 cup of oatmeal with cinnamon and 1 packet of Equal, 1/2 cup of soy milk	✔
		16 ounces of water	✔
	Supplements	Antioxidant Fuel (2 capsules)	✔
		Multivitamin (1 capsule)	✔
10:00 a.m.	**Nutrition Shake**	Myoplex Deluxe (vanilla flavor, blended with 16 oz of water, two ice cubes, and one serving of BetaGen)	✔
11:30 a.m.	**Supplement**	Lean System 7 (3 capsules)	✔
Noon	**Lunch**	Grilled chicken breast	✔
		Baked potato	✔
		Fresh vegetables	✔
		16 ounces of water	✔
3:00 p.m.	**Nutrition Shake**	Myoplex Deluxe (chocolate flavor with one tablespoon of flaxseed oil, blended with 16 ounces of water and two ice cubes)	✔
6:00 p.m.	**Dinner**	Broiled Salmon	✔
		Steamed brown rice	✔
		Steamed spinach	✔
		16 ounces of water	✔
	Supplements	Antioxidant Fuel (2 capsules)	✔
		Multivitamin (1 capsule)	✔
8:30 p.m.	**Protein Drink**	Two scoops of Designer Protein and one serving of BetaGen, mixed with 12 ounces of cold water	✔
9:30 p.m.	**Supplement**	Z-Mass PM (4 capsules)	✔
10:00 p.m.	**Planning Session**	Specifically state my ABSolution Intent for tomorrow's exercise and nutrition Program	✔

On my "worksheet" to the left, you'll notice that on this day, I woke up at 6:00 a.m. The first thing I do after I get up is have a bottle of water, which I keep on an end table next to my bed. And I take three capsules of a supplement called Lean System 7. This supplement contains seven nutrients that have been shown to help the body burn fat at an optimal level, but it does *not* contain ephedra, the popular pep-pill fat burner that I feel better without. The primary ingredient in Lean System 7 is called 7-Keto. It has been shown in scientific studies to increase thyroid hormone activity, which has a significant effect on fat metabolism, especially if you take it first thing in the morning on an empty stomach.

Next, I go downstairs and make a fresh pot of Starbuck's coffee, and I have a cup before I get dressed for my morning workout.

By 6:20 a.m., I was in my home gym, where I did 20 minutes of high-intensity interval training on the StairMaster. On this exercise, I start with a couple minutes to warm up and then crank up the intensity for a minute, then I lower it for 30 seconds, increase it for a minute, and then lower it for 30 seconds, and so on. I increase the intensity a little bit more during each "burst," then I bring it down to a *very* slow climb for my rest periods so I catch my breath.

Fifteen to 20 minutes of HIIT in the morning is a great way to wake up. It increases blood flow, carries oxygen to the brain, warms your body temperature up, which increases your metabolism for much of the day. Also, an intense cardio workout, first thing in the morning, helps me feel calmer and stronger all day long.

After I finish my HIIT workout, I rest for a few minutes, drink a cup of water, and then move onto my ab training. On this day, I did 15 crunches on the Swiss ball, followed immediately by 15 reps of leg lifts on the Swiss ball, followed immediately by 15 repetitions of side crunches, also on the Swiss ball. After I complete a "triple series" (where I do a set of 15 reps for 3 different exercises with no rest inbetween), I take a minute to catch my breath. Then, I do another triple series with the same exercises, rest for another minute, and then do one more.

After my workout, I went upstairs, showered, and got dressed for work. At 7:40 a.m., I was back in my kitchen, this time making my usual breakfast: an omelet with eight egg whites and just a little low-fat cheddar cheese. I also make a small bowl of old-fashioned Quaker oats and serve that with a half cup of soy milk, sweetened with a packet of Equal and a dash of cinnamon. I get my protein from the egg whites and healthy complex carbohydrates from the oatmeal. Along with breakfast, I'll have a 16-ounce bottle of water and a multi-vitamin/mineral capsule.

I'll also consume two antioxidant capsules made by a company called TwinLabs. Antioxidants are vitamins and minerals that have been shown to help neutralize something called free radicals, which are harmful, "out-of-balance" atoms that circulate in our systems, until they are neutralized. A certain amount of antioxidants are produced as a by-product of strenuous exercise, so I think it's important to consume an extra amount of antioxidants to make sure my intense exercise sessions have as much of a health-enhancing effect as possible.

In my journal, you'll see that at 10:00 a.m. I had a Myoplex Deluxe nutrition shake. Remember, it's very important to feed your body with protein, carbohydrates, and the nutrients it needs every two to three hours throughout the day. I've been using Myoplex for over five years, and even though I've tried virtually every nutrition shake on the market, I still believe EAS makes the best one. (For those of you who don't know, I haven't worked for EAS for about three years now, and I'm not getting paid for this "endorsement." Like all the advice in this book, I'm telling you what I actually do—what works for me.) I add a serving of BetaGen to my morning Myoplex. BetaGen is a supplement which contains an effective amount of creatine and HMB; both shown in scientific studies to improve muscle strength and recovery.

At 11:30 a.m. I had three more capsules of Lean System 7. (It works better if you take it on an empty stomach.)

At noon, I had lunch consisting of a grilled chicken breast, baked potato, and fresh vegetables. Remember, what I have done for years is

determine portions by my eyesight. The right portion of protein for me is the size of the palm of my hand. The same for carbohydrates. You can also use smaller plates than what most people use. Anyway, I fill my plate with a third quality protein; a third complex carbohydrates; and a third vegetables. I also have a 16-ounce bottle of water.

At 3:00 p.m., I have another serving of Myoplex Deluxe, this time chocolate flavor with an added tablespoon of flaxseed oil, blended with 16 ounces of water and a couple ice cubes.

I get home from work at 6:00 p.m. and prepare dinner consisting of broiled salmon, brown rice, and steamed spinach. I rarely use salt to enhance the flavor of foods, relying instead on the juice of lemons and limes. Eating healthy, whole foods is not complicated, and once you get used to it, it just feels right. I can't imagine coming home from work and having a bucket of fried chicken. So much of eating preferences is habit, I believe. Anyway, I have another 16-ounce bottle of water with dinner and also take my supplements.

At 8:30 p.m., I have a protein drink made with two scoops of Designer Protein, a supplement I've been using for years. Designer Protein tastes great and it mixes very easily—I stir it with a spoon into 12 ounces of water and add a serving of BetaGen to it.

At 9:30 p.m., I have four capsules of a supplement called Z-Mass PM made by a company called Cytodyne Technologies. This supplement contains the minerals zinc and magnesium and helps me sleep better and has been shown in scientific studies to help increase muscle strength.

At 10:00 p.m., I sit down for a ten-minute planning session and state my ABSolution Intent for the next day.

In addition to all this, I also make sure I get plenty of rest, sleeping about seven hours each night (usually from around 11:00 p.m. to 6:00 a.m.).

That's how I put it all together on that day.

Now, the next day the main difference in my Program is that I did a weight-training workout in the evening, rather than cardio and ab training in the morning. My journal page for that day is on the next page.

ABSolution Worksheet

Name: Shawn Phillips **Date:** May 7

Time	Planned Activity		Status ✔ = Done
6:00 a.m.	16 ounces of water		✔
	Supplement	Lean System 7 (3 capsules)	✔
	Cup of coffee		✔
7:00 a.m.	**Breakfast**	8 egg white omelet with a little low-fat cheddar cheese	✔
		1 cup of oatmeal with cinnamon and 1 packet of Equal, 1/2 cup of soy milk	✔
		16 ounces of water	✔
	Supplements	Antioxidant Fuel (2 capsules)	✔
		Multivitamin (1 capsule)	✔
10:00 a.m.	**Nutrition Shake**	Myoplex Deluxe (vanilla flavor, blended with 16 oz of water, two ice cubes and one serving of BetaGen)	✔
11:30 a.m.	**Supplement**	Lean System 7 (3 capsules)	✔
Noon	**Lunch**	Tuna fish sandwich on whole wheat bread	✔
		with lettuce and tomato	✔
		Steamed carrots	✔
		16 ounces of water	✔
3:00 p.m.	**Nutrition Shake**	Myoplex Deluxe (chocolate flavor with one tablespoon of flaxseed oil, blended with 16 ounces of water and two ice cubes)	✔
6:00 p.m.	**Weight Training**	Chest: Flat Dumbbell Bench—50lb x 15, 65lb x 12, 75lb x 10, 95lb x 8, 100lb x 6	✔
		Incline Dumbbell Flyes— 3 sets: 50lb x 10	✔
		Shoulders: Standing Dumbbell Press—40lb x 12, 50lb x 10, 60lb x 8, 65lb x 6	✔
		Side Raises— 3 sets: 20lb x 10	✔
		Triceps: Lying Dumbbell Extensions— 4 sets: 30lb x 10	✔
		Reverse Grip Extensions— 3 sets: 90lb x 10	✔
8:00 p.m.	**Dinner**	Chicken stir fry	✔
		Steamed vegetables	✔
		Steamed brown rice	✔
		16 ounces of water	✔
	Supplements	Antioxidant Fuel (2 capsules)	✔
		Multivitamin (1 capsule)	✔
10:00 p.m.	**Planning Session**	Specifically state my ABSolution Intent for tomorrow's Program	✔
10:30 p.m.	**Protein Drink**	Two scoops of Designer Protein and one serving of BetaGen, mixed with 12 ounces of cold water	✔
11:00 p.m.	**Supplement**	Z-Mass PM (4 capsules)	✔

On the worksheet to the left, you'll notice that my meals and supplement program look very similar to the previous day. I'm very consistent with my Program. The primary difference is that on this day, I did my weight training in the evening and structured my nutrition and supplementation around that.

As you can see, after I came home from work at 6:00 p.m., I did a weight-training workout that included two exercises for the chest, shoulders, and triceps. I started with the flat dumbbell bench press by doing a warm-up set of 15 reps with a 50-lb dumbbell in each hand. Then I rested about a minute, went up to 65 lbs for 12 reps; 75 lbs for 10 reps; 95 lbs for 8 reps; and then 100 lbs for 6 reps. I focus very intensely during my workout and lower the weights slowly and press the weights up slowly. Most people lift weights way too fast, which not only decreases the effectiveness of the exercise but increases the possibility that they'll suffer a muscle strain or ligament injury.

After the dumbbell bench press, I move onto the incline dumbbell flyes, performing 3 sets of 10 repetitions with 50 lbs. Then I rest a couple minutes before moving onto the standing dumbbell press, which primarily works the shoulder muscles but also the triceps. Since my shoulders are already warmed up from the chest workout, I do a set of 12 repetitions with a 40-lb dumbbell in each hand; 10 repetitions with 50-lb dumbbells; 8 reps with 60-lb dumbbells; and then 6 reps with 65-lb dumbbells. After that, I rest a couple minutes and then do 3 sets of 10 side raises with 20-lb dumbbells. Once again, I rest a minute between each set, and I focus my intensity during each rep of each set. After my shoulder workout, I do two exercises for the triceps. On this day, I did the lying dumbbell triceps extension for 4 sets of 10 reps with 30-lb dumbbells, followed by 3 sets of 10 reps on the reverse grip triceps extension. I used 90 lbs on the weight stack for that exercise.

This weight training workout takes about 40 minutes, and because I keep a quick pace, it is a cardio workout too—my heart rate is up throughout the training session.

I train with weights three times a week. I do chest, shoulders, and triceps for one workout; back, biceps, and legs for the next. Then chest, shoulder, and triceps, and so on. I do my HIIT workouts and ab training three times a week too but on different days. For example, on Monday, Wednesday, and Friday, I'll do HIIT and abs. And on Tuesday, Thursday, and Saturday, I'll train with weights.

I've tried a lot of different weight-training programs over the years, and what I've discovered is if you're using basic free-weight exercises and you're focusing intensely and performing between 6 and 12 repetitions per set, you're going to prime those muscles. Then, if you give the muscles a few days to recover and you feed the body properly, you're going to get results. Weight training isn't nearly as complicated as many people believe. The basics work. The most important thing is to *be consistent and to learn to truly push yourself*, focusing intensely on the muscle being trained. That's the way I've done it, and that's what's worked for me.

Now that you've seen how I put it all together, *it's your turn*. By investing your time and energy in reading and reviewing the information in this book, you're already off to a good start. You're wisely preparing by educating yourself. Of course, this information, by itself, is not going to help you build a better body; it's the *application* of this information that's the real key. So now, it's time to begin *applying* this information! I recommend you start *now* by planning and designing your own ABSolution Program. You'll need a journal, a notebook, a day planner, or you can use the blank ABSolution Worksheet on the next page to help you get started.

Begin by writing down your "ABSolution Intent" for the first day of your Program. When do you intend to work out? Which exercises do you intend to do? What will you eat? What supplements will you take? And when? Make sure all of these questions are answered in specific detail during your planning session. Even plan precisely how long you'll spend working out. By setting a deadline for the amount of time you're allowed to finish your workouts, you'll discover a significant increase in your focused intensity. It's little things like this that can make a big difference.

Once you create your plan, make sure you're prepared. Of course, you'll need to stock your kitchen with the healthy foods and supplements which will nourish your success. And, you'll need to have a gym membership or some basic home-exercise equipment. (I recommend a Swiss ball, an exercise bench, a set of dumbbells, and some basic cardio equipment like a jump rope, StairMaster or stationary bike.)

Another important aspect of proper planning and preparation is to incorporate a level of flexibility into your Program. When things don't go exactly as planned, *have a back-up plan*. For example, if I'm scheduled to have lunch at noon at a local café and my work schedule starts to get in the way, I make sure I have a nutrition bar or nutrition shake nearby. Keep this in mind as you begin the process of planning and preparing for your ABSolution Program.

ABSolution Worksheet

Name:_____ Date:_____

Time	Planned Activity	Status ✔ = Done

I cannot emphasize enough that planning and preparation are vitally important to succeeding on the ABSolution Program. Journaling and keeping track of your ABSolution Intent and also monitoring how closely you were able to follow your plan, each and every day, is perhaps *the* most important exercise you can do. Be honest and accurate with your records. If you have a setback and eat a cheeseburger instead of a grilled chicken breast, just write it down. If you miss a workout, write it down. Then let it go. Instead of worrying about it, vow to do better in the future and move on. Succeeding on the ABSolution Program is about what you do most of the time, not all of the time. *No one will follow this Program perfectly.* Not even I follow this Program perfectly. I do the best I can the vast majority of the time, and the results speak for themselves.

Always remember that to build your best abs, it's not one thing, it's *everything!* As you begin to put all of the principles of the ABSolution Program together—the mindset, nutrition, supplementation, ab training, weight training, and high-intensity cardio—and you begin to *apply* them, day in and day out, you *will* begin to experience positive results! But it won't happen overnight. Give it time; exercise patience as well as common sense, and follow your plan carefully, closely, and consistently. When you do that, *you will succeed!* I promise.

CHAPTER TWELVE

ABSolute Answers to
Frequent Questions

Q: I'm trying to burn the fat off my belly, so I can see my abs. How many sit-ups do I need to do?

A: You *can't* spot reduce fat off your belly or anywhere else for that matter. It's a myth that doing a lot of sit-ups will burn belly fat. It just doesn't work like that.

However, for a moment, let's pretend that spot reduction were possible; that training your abs did help you burn off the belly fat. Now, consider this: scientific research has shown that ten repetitions of sit-ups burns *only* nine calories. Let me help you put this in perspective. Each McDonald's Big Mac with fries and a soft drink contains over 1,300 calories. Again, pretending sit-ups and other abdominal exercises are effective at burning fat, you would have to perform 1,442 sit-ups to burn off the amount of fat and other nutrient-void calories ingested from a single Big Mac lunch. And to burn off just a half pound of stored bodyfat, you'd have to do *over 2,000 sit-ups!*

Clearly, that is not an efficient solution. The *real* solution is to follow a complete, integrated program, like the one I've shared with you in this book.

Q: How low does your bodyfat have to be before you see definition in your midsection? How low is your bodyfat?

A: For guys to start to see definition in their abs—to start to see that six pack—their bodyfat generally has to be below 10%. I usually keep my bodyfat between 6% and 7%. If I go any lower than that, I start to lose energy, and I start to look a little too lean, especially in the face. Remember, I'm 38 years old. I like to have a muscular body, but I want my face to look healthy, too.

Women definitely don't need to get their bodyfat down below 10% to see their abs. Whereas men hold more of their bodyfat in the belly, women often tend to store excess bodyfat more below the waist. Thus, women can see definition in their midsection while their bodyfat is still around 15%.

Q: I have trouble staying motivated. I'll stick with an exercise routine and eat right for a few weeks and then just lose focus and quit. Is there something you could say to keep me motivated to work out and stay with it?

A: Actually, what I have to say about this topic may or may not "motivate" you. The way I see it, motivation is overrated. By that I mean, the ability to get "fired up" or excited about working out and eating foods that support your health isn't the key to sticking with an exercise and nutrition program.

I'm very often not motivated to work out, but I do it anyway. I do it for several reasons. First of all, it's part of who I am—it's part of my authentic character. Also, sticking with an exercise and nutrition program helps me achieve goals I have set for myself, and in that way, each workout and each healthy meal has purpose—it's a step in the direction I've decided to go. Another reason I don't need to rely on motivation to keep me focused on my exercise and nutrition program is that, for me, they're well ingrained habits. And, for most people I know who are in great shape, working out and eating right are habits, not activities they have to get fired up to do.

So, my advice is *don't rely on motivation to keep you going strong*. Set a goal and focus on it every day and visualize yourself achieving that goal. That can help create the inspiration and energy you will need to stay on course during the first month of the ABSolution Program. I've discovered that if people can make it through the first month, they are on their way to developing extremely good fitness habits.

I've got to warn you, though, during that first month, you're going to have to work out when you don't feel like it. And you're going to need to sit down and plan and prepare each and every day of your ABSolution Program, even though you may not feel like doing it.

When it is all said and done, my "motivation" is the *result* of the effort, not the effort itself. That's how it is for me; I suspect it will be that way for you, too.

Q: What's your height, weight, and bodyfat percentage? What about your waist measurement?

A: My height is 5'10"; my weight is 197 lbs (it fluctuates 5 lbs up or down throughout the year). My bodyfat is usually between 6% and 7%. My waist measurement is 31".

Q: What's the difference between your program and Body-*for*-LIFE?

A: The ABSolution Program and Body-*for*-LIFE are more alike than they are different. There's absolutely no disputing the fact that the Body-*for*-LIFE Program works. Literally hundreds of thousands of people have applied it successfully and have turned in their before and after photos as proof of the transformations they've made.

Both my Program and Bill's incorporate a lot of the things we've learned about exercise, nutrition, and supplementation over the past 20 years. In fact, if you look at the principles that support each program, you'll find these aspects in common: both incorporate intense weight training; both involve performing relatively short but highly intense cardiovascular exercise; both include a balanced approach to nutrition and call for you to feed your body frequently throughout the day, and both require a lot of hard work and a positive mindset.

The ABSolution Program incorporates a number of my personal preferences which makes it unique. For example, I don't eat carbohydrates in my last meal each day. That helps me to keep my bodyfat below 7%. Also, I do more ab training than the Body-*for*-LIFE Program recommends. One of the reasons for this is that I've been working out for many years, and my muscles are to the point where they respond better to three ab training sessions per week. I also use more supplements, but once again, this is a personal preference, not something that's absolutely essential to get results.

The bottom line is both Programs are based on tried-and-true fundamentals. Both Programs work!

Q: How long will it take to lose fat and see my abs?

A: On the ABSolution Program, you can expect to lose approximately 10 lbs of fat per month. That's roughly an inch and a half off your waistline per month. So if your goal is to go from a 36" to 32" waistline, you can achieve that in about 3 months of diligent effort.

If your goal is to go from 16% to 8% bodyfat, your program may look like this: after one month, you can expect your bodyfat to be down to about 13%, after two months, your bodyfat percentage could be down to 10%; and after three months, you could have a bodyfat percentage of 8%, which is definitely lean enough to have that ripped look in the midsection.

Of course, the further you have to go, the longer it will take. But with *consistent* effort, you will get there!

Q: Why do you cut carbohydrates after 8:00 p.m.? Isn't it important to have carbohydrates to deliver protein to the muscle cells?

A: Not eating carbohydrates in my sixth meal of the day, which is usually after 8:00 p.m., is something I've been doing for years. What I'm trying to create with the last meal of the day is a "time-released protein" effect. And while it's true that carbohydrates help carry the amino acids from protein into the muscle cells, it's also true that protein, especially the branched-chain amino acids (which there is a high concentration of in my late evening protein drink), help shuttle protein into muscle cells as well. They just do it over a longer period of time. And so with my last meal of the day, I'm looking for a slow effect, so when I'm sleeping, my muscles are being fed for as long as possible, and I maintain what's called a positive-nitrogen balance—an "anabolic" state in the muscles—while I sleep.

Also, I've discovered that after three whole-food meals each day and two nutrition shakes, I'm just not hungry at night. So I have a protein drink and a couple supplements. This is what's worked for me!

Q: Will I get that bloated belly look like a lot of today's bodybuilders have if I work my abs hard?

A: Absolutely not! That distended, bloated gut that many professional bodybuilders have, even when their bodyfat is as low as three or four percent, is not caused by ab training. It is a side effect of the overuse and abuse of bodybuilding drugs. The growth-promoting hormones and anabolic agents that are used in professional bodybuilding today don't just make the muscles grow, they actually increase the size of their internal organs, like the liver, even the heart. When these organs "hypertrophy," the gut distends. Obviously, that is not healthy.

Q: Is it ever a good idea to do longer, low-intensity cardio workouts? I heard that you burn more fat with low-intensity cardio than you do with high-intensity.

A: Some scientific studies show that more fatty acids are broken down and utilized as fuel during a low-intensity workout than with more intense cardio. However, the key is that it's not how many calories or how much fat you burn during your cardio session, *it's how much training increases your metabolism afterwards that makes the difference!*

I totally disregard the "calories burned" read-out on aerobic equipment, like the StairMaster, high-tech stationary bikes, and treadmills. Those machines do not take into consideration that a single session of high-intensity exercise that lasts as little as 10 to 20 minutes can increase your metabolic rate by more than 15% for the 3 hours after the exercise session. Recent studies also show that high-intensity interval training can increase your resting metabolic rate by over 5% for an entire 24-hour period! Low-intensity cardio does not produce that result.

Now, that being said, there are times when I do longer duration, lower intensity aerobic sessions. One of those times is when I'm nursing a sore knee or ankle. In times like this, I need to be very careful about the stress I put on those joints and allow them to heal properly. Also, when I'm getting over a cold or I've been traveling extensively and I can tell my immune system is not at its strongest, I'll do a half hour, sometimes even an hour of relatively low-intensity cardio exercise on the stationary bike, or I'll just go for a two- or three-mile walk. However, those times are the exception, not the rule. And, in fact, they might be considered more "active rest" than serious training.

Q: How do you measure bodyfat?

A: I measure my bodyfat with a simple skin-fold caliper. That's a tool that pinches the skin and the subcutaneous fat right beneath it. Then, using a scientific formula from those skin-fold measurements and factoring in my scale weight, I can calculate my total percentage of bodyfat as well as lean mass. Skin-fold calipers are not expensive and are very useful tools to keep track of your results.

One of the forms of bodyfat testing that I do *not* recommend is bioelectrical impedance (BIA). This is a method of measuring bodyfat that calculates the resistance to an electrical current that runs through your body from one point to another. The concept is sound and scientific, but the results defy common sense. For example, one day I will do a BIA test and my bodyfat will be 7%, the next day, using the same piece of equipment, it can be as high as 20%! For the most part, BIA is BS.

I've also tried hydrostatic weighing, which is the old-fashioned dunk tank "gold standard" of body-composition analysis. It's accurate but highly impractical.

You can't go wrong with a quality set of skin-fold calipers. They can help track your bodyfat and allow you to see how much fat you're losing every month and how much muscle you're gaining. If you visit www.BestABS.com you can find links to where to purchase skin-fold calipers online.

Q: Do you ever count calories? If so, what percentage of the calories in your nutrition program come from carbohydrates, protein, and fat?

A: I don't count calories daily. I don't need to. I know the right amount of food for me when I see it. And, I've been doing this so long I can actually look at a plate of food and tell you, very accurately, how many calories that plate of food contains, including how much is from carbs, protein, and fat.

Generally, I eat about 2,500 calories a day. Of that, 40% or 1,000 calories are from protein (that's 250 grams of protein), about 1,000 calories are from carbohydrates (another 250 grams). And, about 500 calories, or 20% of my daily calorie intake, is from sources of fatty acids (that's about 55 grams of fat).

If your primary goal is to lose bodyfat, you will do well to consume 10 calories per pound of bodyweight per day. If you're just fine tuning and you're already in good shape, shoot for 12 to 14 calories per pound of bodyweight. And, if you're trying to gain muscle and you're not trying to lose fat, 15 to 17 calories per pound of bodyweight per day works well.

However, if you keep track of portions and you eat a balance of carbs and protein, you don't need to count calories.

Q: What about drinking wine with dinner or having beer with some meals—is that all right?

A: A glass or two of wine, once or twice a week, or a couple beers on the weekend is no big deal. However, the daily habit of drinking beer and wine will keep you from making significant progress.

Scientific studies show that the more alcohol a person drinks, the less consistent they are with exercise, and the more unhealthy their eating habits.

Alcohol calories, while technically carbohydrates, aren't an efficient form of energy—your body really doesn't have a whole lot of use for them, so it stores them as bodyfat. (There's a reason they call a beer belly a beer belly!)

Q: How many reps per set does it take to work the ab muscles? I've been doing 5 sets of 50 sit-ups a day. Do I have to do more?

A: No, you don't need to do more sit-ups to get results. It's important to understand that the muscles of the abdominal region are made up primarily of fast-twitch muscle fibers, and they respond very well to relatively low rep sets. I've found that 15 reps per set of most ab exercises works best for me. If you *focus intensely* on each rep, and you do the proper form, 15 reps is plenty.

With most of my other muscle groups, I train between 6 and 12 reps. That's because it's easier to increase the intensity of exercises such as the dumbbell curl, bench press, shoulder press, etc., by increasing the weight you're lifting. With ab training, there aren't a lot of safe and effective ways to increase the intensity by increasing the weight or resistance. That's why it's so important to learn how to properly contract the muscles and focus your intensity.

Q: How often do you change your training program? What about your nutrition program, do you change that too?

A: To keep your body adapting and responding to exercise, you have to vary the intensity or the exercise stress. Otherwise, your body will become accustomed to the training, and you won't get results. That's why many people hit a plateau, even when they're working out hard, they're working out hard in the same way they've been working out hard for a long time.

Incorporating variety into your workouts *is essential*, but it's not complicated. For example, about every month I'll simply rotate exercises to keep my muscles responding—to keep them strong and defined. This can be as simple as changing from doing the flat dumbbell bench press and incline dumbbell flyes for a chest workout to the barbell bench press and flat dumbbell flyes. Also, you can simply change the order of the exercises. If you've been doing a barbell bench press first in your workout, followed by incline dumbbell flyes, after a month, you can do the incline dumbbell flyes first, followed by the bench press. This forces different muscles to be recruited and primed during a workout. You can also increase the weight you're lifting to continually prime the muscles. And you can vary the number of sets and reps.

I vary my cardio workouts as well. I have a lot of different cardio routines I like, including hill climbing, sprinting/jogging, and stair climbing outdoors. I'm also conscious not to develop the habit of just doing one type of aerobic exercise machine indoors, such as the stationary bike, StairMaster, etc. A lot of people find exercises they're comfortable with and then they fall into a rut—they develop the habit (which becomes a bad habit) of doing the same exercises, with the same weight, at the same intensity. I want to emphasize again, this is one of the things that causes plateaus. To continue to get results, you have to continue to incorporate *variety*, as well as *increased intensity*, into your workout program.

Now, it doesn't work that way with nutrition. For me, I eat essentially the same foods, day after day, week after week. There's no reason to incorporate variety into your nutrition program for physiological reasons, although some people find that it is psychologically helpful to vary the foods they're eating, so they don't get bored with their good healthy whole foods and be tempted to eat unhealthy fat and sugar-fortified fast foods and junk foods.

Q: How do women build their best abs?

A: The same way guys do! It's a combination of the right mindset, proper nutrition, supplementation, ab training, weight training, and intense cardio. I recommend the same program for women as I do for men. Of course, women are not going to develop as much muscle definition as men, simply because of the fact that their hormone levels are different, and therefore, they respond differently to weight training.

Q: What are your favorite foods? Which foods do you never eat?

A: My favorite foods and the ones I stock my kitchen with include lean sources of protein, such as chicken breasts, salmon, halibut, sea bass, tuna, nonfat cottage cheese, eggs, eggs, and more eggs. My favorite sources of complex carbohydrates include brown rice, potatoes, yams, whole-wheat pasta (which I eat only once a week because I have a tendency to get carried away and eat too much of it), and whole-wheat bread (which I also eat sparingly). I also stock my kitchen with vegetables, such as broccoli, squash, red and green peppers, carrots, peas, green beans, and tomatoes. I keep a lot of steamed vegetables in Tupperware containers in my refrigerator, so when I feel like snacking, I reach for those instead of the traditional snack foods like crackers, cookies, and other carbohydrate crap. For fruit, I like apples, bananas (which I often add to my nutrition shakes), grapefruit, and oranges. Usually, I have one piece of fruit a day.

Foods I rarely, if ever, bring into my house include donuts, pastries, cookies, ice cream, chips, crackers, high-sugar cereals, white bread, bagels, meat from a deli (which is usually higher in fat than the label says and loaded with sodium), and peanut butter.

What I've learned is that *if I don't want to wear it on my belly, I don't buy it at the grocery store!* For example, donuts don't look good on me. Fresh vegetables, healthy carbohydrates, lean sources of quality protein... those foods, I wear well.

For me, kitchen management is a big part of succeeding, over the long term. Having unhealthy foods in your kitchen, waiting there for even a brief moment of "weakness" is a formula for failure. I suggest that the next time you're in your kitchen, open your cabinets, refrigerator, and freezer, and step back and take a look at what you've got there. Think about which foods are going to help you succeed and which ones are going to get in your way. Then get rid of foods that are working against you. And stock your kitchen with healthy foods that nourish your success. This is a very important exercise. Remember, building your best abs involves as much training in the kitchen as it does in the gym!

Q: Do you use a fat-burner supplement that contains ephedra and caffeine?

A: I've read and reviewed the scientific studies that show the relatively potent fat-burning effects of ephedra, especially when it's combined with caffeine. And I've tried the caffeine/ephedra "stack" with mixed results. I did notice some fat loss, but it felt like I was taking my central nervous system on a rollercoaster ride. This stuff is unpredictable. Sometimes I'd be "amped up" for a couple hours and then crash. Other times the stuff wouldn't even "kick in" until I was getting ready to go to bed! Granted, that's only my experience. For some people, using thermogenic fat burners with ephedra in them seems to work. However, the fact that so many people are using these supplements and relying on them as a quick fix... often taking more than the recommended dose, is especially concerning and can be dangerous.

I understand why people would want to take a supplement that helps them burn fat; after all, there is no way you're going to see definition in your abdominal muscles, regardless of how much ab training you do, if you don't do something to get rid of that fat. Fortunately, there are supplements, besides ephedra, that have been scientifically shown to upgrade your body's ability to burn fat. One of the most intriguing supplements, which I've been using for the past six months, is called *7-Keto*. (It's the primary ingredient in a new product called *Lean System 7*.) I learned about this nutrient from a medical doctor named John Zenk, who's a board certified doctor of internal medicine with over 20 years of clinical experience. His research on 7-Keto shows that it may significantly decrease bodyweight and bodyfat without the detrimental side effects found with so many of the stilmulant-based formulas. Unlike ephedra, *7-Keto does not have an effect on the central nervous system*. Plus, it significantly increases your body's ability to burn fat, especially when combined with an effective exercise and nutrition program. The findings on 7-Keto are the result of over 10 years of diligent work in the lab and $8 million invested in scientific research. The research has shown that this supplement is extremely effective at activating a type of thyroid hormone called "T3," which is produced by the body naturally and plays a very important role in fat burning. In fact, if your levels of this thyroid hormone are low, you'll often have an extremely difficult time losing bodyfat, even when you're exercising and eating right. By taking a supplement to naturally upregulate the activity of this hormone, it's been shown that the metabolic rate can be increased quite significantly. Scientific studies also show that test subjects who used 7-Keto and followed a nutrition and exercise program *lost three times as much bodyfat* after eight weeks with 7-Keto compared to the test subjects who followed the *same* nutrition and exercise program but did *not* use the supplement.

Because I am extremely impressed with the potential of Lean System 7 and 7-Keto, and because I believe it is very important that people find a safer alternative to all the ephedra-based fat burners, I'm doing what I can to help educate people about it, and I'm partnering with a new company called iSatori Global Technologies, Inc., to help distribute Lean System 7. If you'd like to learn more about this new supplement and evaluate the research behind it, visit www.leansystem7.com.

Q: Are nutrition bars any good? If so, which ones do you use?

A: I think nutrition shakes are much better than nutrition bars as they generally have higher quality protein, and they're easier on the gut. I'll eat a nutrition bar once in a while but never more than one a day. Usually I have a nutrition bar only about once or twice a week.

I carry a few nutrition bars with me when I travel, so if I get stuck on an airplane and my choice is a nutrition bar or Delta Airline's mystery meat, I'll have a healthy back-up plan. My favorite bars are the ones made by Next Protein and EAS' Myoplex bars.

Q: The most confusing thing about getting in shape for me is keeping track of which supplements work and which ones don't. How can I stay up to date?

A: Keeping track of what's real and what's a gimmick in today's supplement market is a challenge. Many people are getting ripped off because they don't know the facts before they buy. That's the main reason I've been working for years on the development of Nutros.com, which is an online supplement guide with one of the world's largest research libraries supporting it. Virtually any question you have about supplements can be answered at Nutros.com. When you visit Nutros.com, be sure to sign up to receive my free online newsletter, which can help you get the facts about what works and what doesn't, when it comes to nutritional supplements.

Q: I've been working out hard, dieting, and not making gains. What should I do?

A: I know how frustrating it can be when you're really giving it your best effort, but you feel like you're not getting anywhere. Trust me, I've been there. For me, the most important thing in times like this is that I maintain a healthy mindset. If I become obsessed or stressed out because I don't perceive that I'm making gains, that can become a serious problem.

When I start to get that feeling I'm working hard but going nowhere, I don't immediately start slashing calories from my nutrition program or exercising more, which is a mistake many people make. Instead, I focus on something positive. I shift my mindset so I perceive every single workout as a success! I see every time I have a nutrition shake and take my supplements as another success! During these times, I shift my focus away from my physical condition and pay close attention my good habits, and I journal carefully. I write down things like, "Today *I succeeded again* by eating nutritious foods and working out hard!"

Also, I analyze my program, going back through my journal records to see if anything stands out—if it's time to incorporate more variety into my weight training; if I've been eating often enough; if I've been eating the right foods, etc. One of the extremely helpful things about journaling is it allows you to go back and analyze what you've been doing. Oftentimes, you'll find areas where you can make improvements. But if you have no journal and no records, it's extremely hard to do this.

Above all else, I recommend you *stay positive* and not give up! Sometimes changes are not noticeable on a daily basis. But if you stick with it, the changes accumulate and become very dramatic.

Q: How do you stay on your diet when you go out to eat? Do you eat out at restaurants?

A: First of all, *I don't diet.* To me, dieting has a very negative connotation, and it implies a temporary state where you sacrifice and basically employ willpower in an effort to not eat. Dieting, or restricting calories, as a way to lose weight and get in shape is like trying to hold your

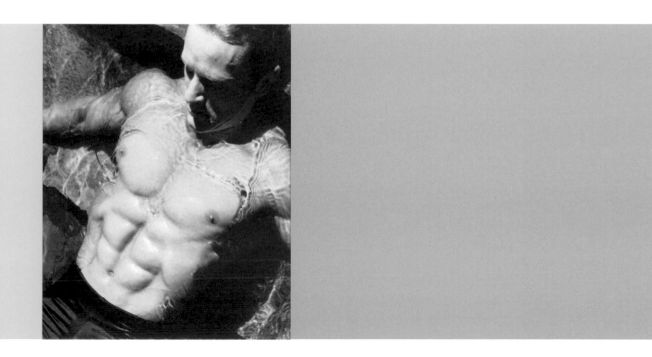

breath—no matter how hard you try, eventually your willpower's going to give out and you're going to open your mouth again. My approach to nutrition is to *feed my body*, not starve it! So I don't call the way I eat "dieting."

Now, how do you nourish your success when you're not eating at home? Well, that's not complicated at all. When you go out to eat, learn to ask for foods the way you know you need them. It's not hard at all to get a chicken breast, baked potato, and steamed vegetables at a restaurant. Just ask for it, even if it's not on the menu. And learn to recognize what is an appropriate portion. One of the biggest problems with going out to eat is that restaurants usually serve oversized portions. Oftentimes, when my food is served, I "downsize" the portion and set whatever I don't need on a separate plate. I do this before I start eating.

Basically, when you go out to eat, apply the same principles you would if you were eating at home. Control the portions, eat quality, lean sources of protein and healthy complex carbohydrates and vegetables and drink a lot of water.

Q: I've never seen my abs. A person training at the gym said some people have them, and some people don't. Is that true?

A: Make no mistake, *you've got abs*. Everybody does! Now, of course, each person's genetics will, to some extent, determine what their abs look like. But we've all got them, and they are skeletal muscles and can be developed.

Some people assume that my abs are there merely because of genetics. The fact is, genetics give us the potential, but it's hard work and dedication that allow us to maximize our genetic potential, whether it's to build great abs or cultivate excellence in any area.

When I was a judge for the Body-*for*-LIFE Challenge a few years ago, I witnessed thousands of extraordinary "ab transformations." The number of people who had big bellies and no definition who transformed so much that they looked like they could be modeling for the cover of *Men's Health* magazine in just three months was even surprising to me. There are people everywhere who are doing it, and *it is possible*.

Q: Have you ever had liposuction on your abs? Is that what people are doing to get such great abs?

A: No, I've never had liposuction on my abs. But, a lot of people have tried it; in fact, last year liposuction was the most popular cosmetic surgery in America, with over 750,000 procedures performed. That's up tenfold (no pun intended) over the past decade. (Less than 70,000 liposuction surgeries were performed in 1990.)

Liposuction is a procedure where doctors make small cuts in the skin near the area where you want to remove fat and then stick a tube, or "cannula," under the skin to break up fat cells and suck it out with a vacuum pump or large syringe. The state-of-the-art method of liposuction includes using a cannula that produces "ultrasonic" energy, which explodes the walls of the fat cells and liquefies them. This generally takes longer and is more expensive than traditional liposuction but is being used more and more frequently.

Risks involved with liposuction include infection, fat and/or blood clots (which can be deadly if they move into the lungs, where they can cause an embolism), friction burns, perforation of vital organs, as well as adverse reactions to anesthetics that are used during the surgery. While the risks are minimized by working with a competent, experienced medical doctor, liposuction is still a serious medical procedure. It is also expensive, averaging over $3,000 per treatment.

I've talked to quite a few people who have tried liposuction. And, I've seen the results on their bodies. Overall, I'm not impressed. Most of these people could have achieved better results had they just followed a smart exercise and nutrition program for a few months. And *none of them* developed defined abdominal muscles! More than half of them gained back

the weight they had sucked out. You see, the big problem with liposuction is that it doesn't treat the bad habits that cause the fat gain to begin with. And even though liposuction removes fat cells from the area that's treated, it does not prevent your body from storing that fat in other areas. For example, if someone had liposuction on their "love handles" and they reduced the amount of fat stored in that area but they continued to do what they were doing, which caused them to gain fat before, they simply store more fat in their lower back, belly, and hips. How wonderful... trade one problem area for another!

Another reason people are often disappointed with the results of liposuction is that it can only remove subcutaneous bodyfat—that's the bodyfat that's right under the skin. What many people don't realize is that "beer belly look" (which many guys have) or "pooch" in the lower belly (that women are often frustrated by) is caused by bodyfat that is stored *inside* the gut, between the organs. This internal fat can only be burned off through exercise and proper nutrition—this fat can't be sucked out, and until it's gone, you won't have a flat belly. Also, when the abdominal muscles are weak and not properly conditioned, the belly won't be flat and firm.

Clearly, hard work in the gym and eating right is the smarter approach.

Q: What's the best target heart rate to burn fat during my cardio workouts?

A: The general recommendation is that people perform aerobic exercise at roughly 70% of their maximum heart rate to burn fat. A person's maximum heart rate is said to be 220 minus their age. For example, for me, this formula shows that my maximum heart rate is 182 beats per minute (220 minus 38 [my age]). And, 70% of that is about 130 heart beats per minute. Now, once again, according to the general recommendation, you should maintain this heart rate for at least 20 minutes to stimulate effective fat burning.

I don't think it's a bad idea to monitor your heart rate during exercise, but I also don't think it's necessary. If you're pushing yourself during high-intensity intervals with your cardio, you know when your heart rate is up. When you're breathing hard, you're working out hard. I try not to make it any more complicated than that.

There isn't really a scientific formula to determine if you're exercising with the proper intensity. That's something you have to reach deep down inside and answer for yourself. During your workouts, if you're pushing yourself *as hard as you can*, you're exercising intensely! If you're slacking or holding back, you're *not* exercising intensely.

Now, for one person, an intense workout might be bench pressing 150 lbs for 10 reps. For someone else, it might be pressing 300 lbs for 10 reps. Intensity might be me literally sprinting up a flight of stairs during a HIIT workout. For someone else, it might be walking up those stairs. Intensity is different for every person. You can't measure it with a stopwatch nor heart-rate monitor.

Q: What's the best ab-exercise equipment? I've got an Ab Energizer belt. Have you tried that?

A: I've tried virtually every ab exercise training device you can think of, including your "Ab Energizer." That device is based on something called "electrical muscle stimulation" or EMS. EMS has been used for years by physical therapists and athletic trainers in an effort to help rehabilitate muscles after injury or surgery. EMS can prevent muscle atrophy by electrically stimulating a contraction in a muscle, for example, the quadriceps of the thigh, during a period when that muscle has to be immobilized following knee surgery. When used properly by a physical therapist, EMS can help reduce recovery time, so an athlete can get back on the playing field faster.

However, the battery-operated EMS belts, which are so popular today (with millions of these devices sold over the last couple years alone) are no more effective than doing simple floor crunches. And certainly, they are hardly responsible for the rock-hard abs displayed on the models wearing the belts in the popular TV ads. Make no mistake, those bodies were built with a complete exercise program, including weight training, cardiovascular exercise, and proper nutrition.

A recent study at San Diego State University took a scientific look at many of the other ab-training devices which are so popular today. The scientists hooked up electrodes to a group of test subjects to measure how hard the various abdominal muscles were working while they were performing ab exercises, both with and without the machines. These scientists showed that most of the devices, including the popular Torso Track, produced about the same amount of contraction as a set of floor crunches. The study also showed that the Ab Rocker was half as effective as regular floor crunches. The *most* muscle activation was experienced by the test subjects when they performed ab exercises on a Swiss ball!

The bottom line is most of these ab machines are over-hyped gimmicks. You're better off learning basic ab exercises and developing the skill to apply focused intensity. Beyond that, the best exercise device you can get is a Swiss ball, which is available at many sporting goods and gym equipment stores. Also, you can visit www.BestABS.com and I'll direct you to online retailers who sell Swiss balls. They're very inexpensive—less than $40 for a top-quality one.

Q: I don't have time to work out. Can I get results by just dieting?

A: I repeat, I don't recommend "dieting." I recommend people learn how to feed their bodies properly! Virtually everyone has time to exercise. Who doesn't have at least 20 minutes a day to improve their health, enhance the quality and length of their life, and enjoy looking and feeling better? One of the best ways to create time for exercise is to simply get up a half hour earlier than you normally do and exercise at home. *It's that simple.*

Q: Do I have to have a workout partner or trainer to do the ABSolution Program?

A: Working together with a friend, spouse, co-worker, or even someone you might meet at the gym who has similar goals can help. In fact, scientific studies have shown that people who work out with a partner get better results faster. But that doesn't mean you need to wait for somebody else to help you out. You can succeed on the ABSolution Program no matter what! Consider *me* your workout partner.

Q: If I have more questions, how can I contact you?

A: It's an honor and a pleasure to help you out in any way I can! I can be reached at www.BestABS.com where I'll be frequently updating information and answering even more questions about the ABSolution Program. Please visit me online any time you need help. I'll do whatever I can to support you in your efforts to build a healthier, stronger body, complete with *your* own absolutely fantastic abs!